BARRON'S

Painless
Grammar

FIFTH EDITION

Rebecca Elliott, Ph.D.

Dedication

This book is for Josh
and
Isabela, Sofia, Brinley, and Kayla
and
Bill, Emily, Syman, Katie, Marshall, Hartley, Becca,
Tori, Wesley, David, Ryan, Parker, Kate, Meg,
Kristopher, Austin, Kacey, Tucker, Miranda
and
Archer, Charlie, Lydia, Sutton, Satie, Julianne, James, Lela,
Branch, Sawyer, Levi, Annabelle, Henry, Phoebe, Laney,
Ella Kate, Joe, Maryanne, Finley, Davis, Henry, Mimi, Cash, Lily
and
all other kids who want to learn to write right
without being bored to death in the process.

Published by Kaplan, Inc., d/b/a Barron's Educational Series
750 Third Avenue
New York, NY 10017
www.barronseduc.com

ISBN: 978-1-5062-6810-1

10 9 8 7 6 5 4 3 2 1

Barron's Educational Series, Inc. print books are available at special quantity
discounts to use for sales promotions, employee premiums, or educational purposes. For more information or to purchase books, please call the Simon & Schuster
special sales department at 866-506-1949.

Contents

How to Use This Book

Painless Grammar is a user-friendly, action-packed, fun-filled book for those who want to learn to write well without atrophying their brains from boredom.

I hope this book will help you write better and help students get higher grades in language arts and English class, but much more importantly, I hope it will help unleash your creativity, set your imagination on fire, and show you the pleasure that can come from expressing your ideas with clarity and style.

Painless Icons and Features

This book is designed with several unique features to help make learning grammar easy.

You will see Painless Tips throughout the book. These include helpful tips, hints, and strategies on the surrounding topics.

Caution boxes will help you avoid common pitfalls or mistakes. Be sure to read them carefully.

REMINDER

Reminders will call out information that is important to remember. Each reminder will relate to the current chapter or will reference key information you learned in a previous chapter.

 **BRAIN TICKLERS**

There are Brain Ticklers throughout each chapter in the book. These quizzes are designed to make sure you understand what you've just learned and to test your progress as you move forward in the chapter. Complete all the Brain Ticklers and check your answers. If you get any wrong, make sure to go back and review the topics associated with the questions you missed.

EXAMPLES

There are examples throughout the book to help you identify sentences that are "Wrong" and "Right," "Weak" and "Better," and more to help you grasp grammar rules and to improve your writing.

SIDEBARS

These shaded boxes contain extra information that relates to the surrounding topics. Sidebars can include advanced topics, detailed examples, and more to help keep grammar interesting and painless.

Chapter 1

Parts of Speech

Every player on a football team has a specific role to play in the game. The quarterback has one job, the linebackers have another job, and the tackles have yet another job. Similarly, every instrument in the school band has its own unique sound, and the music you hear is created by all those different instruments blending together and working together.

Just as the players on the football team or the instruments in the band have their specific jobs, every word in a sentence has its particular job and plays its special role. There are eight parts of speech, and every word in every sentence is playing one of those eight roles.

The eight parts of speech are nouns, pronouns, verbs, adjectives, adverbs, conjunctions, prepositions, and interjections.

Many words almost always play one particular role, but sometimes they can switch roles. The word *boy*, for example, is almost always a noun. However, if you say, "Oh boy, what lousy weather," *oh boy* is an interjection. The word *foot* is almost always a noun, but it plays the role of an adjective if you're talking about a *foot-long* sandwich. The word *fly* is a noun if you're talking about a buzzing insect, but it's a verb if you're talking about *flying* in an airplane. Knowing what part of speech a word is playing helps us understand how sentences are made and also helps us avoid some very common, and sometimes very funny, goofs.

Let's explore the parts of speech and some of the mistakes that students often make with them.

Noun Pointers

What is a noun?

It is a word that names a person, place, thing, idea, or quality.

Person	boy, teacher, Josh, doctor, mother
Place	Miami, city, countryside, United States
Thing	house, tree, horse, bicycle, ice cream
Idea	democracy, truth, illusion, fantasy
Quality	beauty, caring, boredom, silliness

We use <u>nouns</u> all the <u>time</u> when we write <u>e-mails</u> to <u>friends</u> or <u>papers</u> for <u>class</u>. (For <u>example</u>, all these underlined <u>words</u> are <u>nouns</u>.) In the next few <u>pages</u>, we'll look at some <u>mistakes</u> that <u>students</u> frequently make with <u>nouns</u>—and I'll give you <u>pointers</u> on how to avoid making those <u>mistakes</u> when you write.

When to capitalize nouns

Names of specific people

CAPS:

Tucker, Lola, Juanita, Denzel, the Stevens family, the Joneses

NO CAPS:

family, boy, girl, sister, cousin
(These are general groups or categories, not specific people.)

What about mom and dad? Capitalize them when you're calling your parent's name but not when you refer to "my mom" or "my dad."

CAPS:

Hi, Mom! Welcome home, Dad.

NO CAPS:

My father and my mother are busy. Could your mom or your dad drive us to the mall?

Days of the week, months, and holidays, but not seasons

CAPS:

Monday, December, Passover, Easter

NO CAPS:

autumn, fall, spring, winter, summer

Ranks and titles, but only when used right before a particular person's name

CAPS:

This is Doctor Smith, this is Aunt Anne, and that man is General Bradshaw.

NO CAPS:

That man is my doctor, that woman is my aunt, and that man is a general in the army.

CAPS AND NO CAPS:

Our beloved Principal Valentine announced that all teachers and principals in our city get next week off!

What about the president? Many people think the word *president* (or *pope* or *queen*) is so important that they capitalize it all the time. To some people this may look respectful, but to many others it looks unnecessary or even wrong. Always use a capital *P* if the word *president* comes right before the president's name (in other words, if it's being used as part of the person's title). Otherwise, ask yourself if you really need that capital letter.

CAPS:

Everybody greeted President Barack Obama warmly.

NO CAPS:

The former president Barack Obama threw out the first ball of the World Series.

Geographic areas: cities, states, countries, counties, rivers, oceans, streets, parks, etc.

CAPS:

North Dakota, Ohio River, Atlantic Ocean, Franklin Street, Central Park, Lake Jordan, Rocky Mountains

NO CAPS:

The ocean is deep. The mountains are high.

Regions of the United States, but not simple directions

CAPS:

I was born in the Midwest, but I grew up in the North.

NO CAPS:

I live on the north side of town.

Historical periods and events

CAPS:

the Renaissance, World War II, the Middle Ages, the Civil War, the Boston Tea Party

NO CAPS:

It was a long war. We live in an age of computers.

Religions, nationalities, and races of people

CAPS:

Christians, Jews, Buddhists, Muslims, Asians, Africans, Chinese, African Americans

NO CAPS:

There are many churches, temples, and mosques in our city, and they are attended by people of many different races.

Languages, countries, and adjectives related to those countries

CAPS:

Denmark, Danish art, Germany, German exchange student

NO CAPS:

french fries, venetian blinds, brussels sprouts, roman numerals (Some phrases have become so common in our language that the cap is being used less often. It's not wrong to use a cap with these phrases, but ask yourself if you really need it. Are roman numerals just used in Rome? Are french fries unique to France? If you don't really need a cap, don't use it.)

The various names for God and the names of sacred books

CAPS:

God, Jehovah, Allah, the Bible, the Koran

NO CAPS:

There were many gods and goddesses in ancient myths.

Specific school courses, but not general subjects unless they are languages

CAPS:

I'm taking Algebra 101 and History of Ancient China.

CAPS AND NO CAPS:

I'm taking algebra, history, and French.

Names of specific schools, businesses, buildings, organizations, hospitals, churches

CAPS:

Apple Computer, Phillips Middle School, the University of Vermont, United States Capitol, World Health Organization

NO CAPS:

I want a new computer. That building is a middle school.

Brand names

CAPS:

Chevrolet Camaro, Nintendo, Cheerios, Nestle's Crunch

Names of planets, but not sun and moon and sometimes not earth

CAPS:

Saturn has 62 moons; Mars has two moons; Earth has only one lonely moon. (Earth is capitalized when you're referring to it as one of the planets or including it with other capitalized planets.)

NO CAPS:

The moon is full tonight, shining down on the more than six billion people who live on the earth. (The word *earth* is not capitalized when you use the word *the* and talk about *the earth*.)

Names of specific teams and clubs and their members

CAPS:

the Atlanta Braves, the Republican Party, Republicans

NO CAPS:

I play on a baseball team. She is a member of a political party.

Titles of movies, books, chapters, and articles

CAPS:

Harry Potter and the Sorcerer's Stone, "Tar Heels Beat Duke 102–96," *Diary of a Wimpy Kid*

NO CAPS:

Capitalize every word in a title except for these:

- the articles *a*, *an*, and *the*
- the conjunctions *and*, *but*, *for*, *or*, *yet*, *so*, and *nor*
- the words *to* and *as*
- all prepositions (short ones such as *in* and *with* as well as long ones such as *throughout* and *without*); see page 50 for more information about words that look like prepositions but are not
- Do capitalize any word that is the first or last word of the title or that is the first word after a dash or colon. I love the book *The Best Treat of All: A New Puppy to Play With*.

PAINLESS TIP

BEWARE OF THE CAP TRAP

Some people get Carried Away with Caps. They seem to think that every Word they capitalize suddenly becomes Exciting or Important. Don't fall into the Cap Trap. CRAZY CAPS make your work look Very, Very Bad.

Making nouns possessive

When we want to show that someone owns something, we use possessive nouns.

The nose of Mary = Mary's nose
The toes of Gary = Gary's toes

To make a noun possessive, usually add an apostrophe and an *s*.

Noun	Possessive
Sofia	Sofia's cat
cat	the cat's tail
Boris	Boris's mustache

In the past, exceptions to this rule were old-fashioned or historical names, or names that end with an *iz* or *eez* sound:

RIGHT:

Moses' tablets
Achilles' heel
Jesus' parables

ALSO RIGHT:

Jesus's parables (In modern writing, this is considered also correct because we pronounce the word with the extra *s*—Jesus-es—so it is correct if you wish to add the apostrophe and *s*. Achilles ends with an *eez* sound and Moses ends with an *iz* sound. Pronouncing the *es* sounds silly, so we don't add the apostrophe and *s* to those names.)

If two people own the same thing, use an apostrophe and *s* for only the second person.

Syman and Mimi's marriage (they share one marriage)
Kate and Meg's father (they share one father)

If the two people don't own the same thing, use an apostrophe and *s* for both people.

Syman's and Mimi's toes (they don't share the same toes)
Kate's and Meg's teeth (they don't share the same teeth)

Showing possession when the noun is plural

If the plural ends in *s* (for example, *boys*) just add an apostrophe. If the plural does not end in *s* (for example, *women*) add an apostrophe and an *s*.

One person, one item	Two people, two items
the boy's jacket	the boys' jackets
my parent's car	my parents' cars
my boss's hat	my bosses' hats
the woman's dress	the women's dresses
the child's toy	the children's toys

Inanimate objects usually don't own things, but some possessives are okay.

one month's vacation	two months' vacation
one dollar's worth	two dollars' worth
the razor's edge	the two razors' edges
the chair's leg	the chairs' legs

What about the example *the chair's leg*? It's okay, but in formal writing it should be *the chair leg* or *the leg of the chair*. The same is true with this example:

OKAY:

my bike's tire

BETTER:

my bike tire (I own the tire—the bike doesn't own it.)

ALSO GOOD:

the tire on my bike

CAUTION—Major Mistake Territory!

Proper nouns (people's names) that end in s can scramble your brain.

Here's the key:

> Mr. and Mrs. Jones have a new car.
> The Joneses have a new car.
> Mr. Jones's car is new.
> The Joneses' car is new.

PAINLESS TIP

Check this out:

The kid's bike = one kid, one bike
The kids' bike = two (or more) kids sharing the same bike
The kids' bikes = two (or more) kids with different bikes

Making nouns plural

One book, two <u>books</u>, one hat, two <u>hats</u>—what's the big deal? We make <u>words</u> plural all the time. So you think <u>plurals</u> are a piece of cake? Most are, but look at some of these <u>troublemakers</u>:

If it's Why is it	house—houses mouse—mice	If it's Why is it	box—boxes ox—oxen
If it's Why is it	hero—heroes banjo—banjos	If it's Why is it	safe—safes knife—knives
If it's Why is it	cupful—cupfuls passerby—passersby	Go figure:	child—children man—men woman—women

A few nouns stay the same no matter whether you're talking about one of them or a thousand of them. Check these out:

Singular	Plural	Singular	Plural
moose	moose	sheep	sheep
deer	deer	series	series
species	species	swine	swine

The plurals of some words are based on rules from foreign languages; you either have to memorize them or look them up.

Singular	Plural	Singular	Plural
basis	bases	nucleus	nuclei
crisis	crises	stimulus	stimuli
criterion	criteria	analysis	analysis

RULES FOR EASY (REGULAR) PLURALS

Usually add s:
wave—waves
hat—hats

If the word ends in o, usually add es:
hero—heroes
potato—potatoes
exceptions: tattoos, hippos, radios, banjos

If the word ends in s, x, z, ch, or sh, add es:
glass—glasses
church—churches
box—boxes
bush—bushes
buzz—buzzes

If the word ends in y and there's a vowel (a, e, i, o, or u) before the y, add s:
play—plays
monkey—monkeys

If the word ends in y and there's a consonant before the y, change the y to i and add es:
party—parties
candy—candies

If a proper noun (someone's name) ends in y, just add s:
the Kennedy family—the Kennedys
the Finley family—the Finleys

If a compound noun (a noun containing more than one word) has a main noun in it, add the s to the main noun:
one father-in-law, two fathers-in-law
one chief of police, two chiefs of police

If a compound noun has no main noun in it, add the s at the end:
one follow-up, two follow-ups
one trade-in, two trade-ins

Just for fun

If this is right	one die, two dice
Then why shouldn't we say	one pie, two pice
And	one lie, two lice
If this is right	one mouse, two mice
Then why shouldn't we say	one spouse, two spice
If this is right	one cherub, two cherubim
Then why shouldn't we say	one bathtub, two bathtubim
If this is right	one foot, two feet
Then why shouldn't we say	one root, two reet
And	one boot, two beet
If this is right	one goose, two geese
Then why shouldn't we say	one moose, two meese

If this is right	one man, two men
Then why shouldn't we say	one pan, two pen
And	one fan, two fen
And	one can, two cen
If this is right	one tooth, two teeth
Then why shouldn't we say	one telephone booth, two telephone beeth

BRAIN TICKLERS   Set # 1

Find the goofs in these sentences and correct them.

1.   Lucas' house is next door to Bill Gates' house; I bet he gets a lot of hand-me-down computers!

2.   Lily is captain of the girl's softball team.

3.   The womans' dress is made of silk.

4.   Marshall and David's fingers were nearly frostbitten after playing in the snow for three hours.

5.   I asked dad to drive me to Maryanne's house.

6.   The Earth is home to dozens of species of Monkeys, more types of Fungi and Mushrooms than we can count, and many fascinating creatures living deep in the Ocean that we have yet to discover.

7.   I heard the babie's cries.

8.   I borrowed my bosses car for an hour because mine was in the shop.

9.   I grew up in the south.

10. The City where Batman lives is Gotham City.

11. There are two James's and three Mindies in my class this year.

(Answers are on pages 52–53.)

Pronoun Pointers

What is a pronoun?

It is a word that stands in for a noun. (The word *pro* in Latin means "for.") Pronouns are handy little critters. If you don't believe me, let's try talking without them.

GIMME A BREAK:

Isabela gave Isabela's dog the dog's bath.

MUCH SIMPLER:

Isabela gave <u>her</u> dog <u>its</u> bath.

GIMME A BREAK:

Please say the name of the person on the other end of this telephone.

MUCH SIMPLER:

<u>Who</u> are <u>you</u>? <u>What</u> is <u>your</u> name?

GIMME A BREAK:

The person named Katie sitting in that chair likes the person named Satie sitting in that chair.

MUCH SIMPLER:

<u>She</u> likes <u>her</u>.

Here are the ways we use pronouns:

- to name specific people or things: <u>You</u> look like <u>him</u>.
- to point to non-specific people or things: <u>Everyone</u> enjoyed the party, but <u>nobody</u> remembered to thank the hostess.
- to point to some particular thing: <u>This</u> is the dress I want.
- to show mutual action: Ryan and Wesley were wrestling and hurt <u>each other</u>.
- to ask a question: <u>Who</u> doesn't love pronouns?
- to show ownership: That's not <u>yours</u>—it's <u>mine</u>!
- to refer back to the subject: Bruce hurt <u>himself</u>.
- to add emphasis: I <u>myself</u> love pronouns.

PAINLESS TIP

The "self" pronouns (myself, yourself, himself, herself, itself, oneself, ourselves, yourselves, themselves) are used for the two purposes above only: for emphasis and to "double back" to the person doing the action. (See page 165 for more on the ways people often use *myself* incorrectly.)

Do you see how all of the underlined words above stand in for nouns? Let's say that Ella Kate likes Julianne. <u>She</u> likes <u>her</u>. *She* stands in for the noun "Ella Kate," and *her* stands in for the noun "Julianne."

If I say to you, "Please take <u>this</u> to <u>him</u>," the word *this* stands in for the noun "apple" or "bologna sandwich" or whatever it is I'm handing to you. The word *him* stands in for the noun "Phillip" or "Henry" or "Trent" or whomever I'm asking you to take it to.

<u>We</u> can't always use nouns and <u>we</u> often need a simple little word to stand in for a whole lot of words. Imagine that I weren't allowed to use the word *we* in the previous sentence. I'd have to write out the names of every single person in the world! That one little word *we* saves a whole lot of writing.

And what if you don't know exactly <u>whom</u> you're talking about? The word *who* or *whom* could be standing in for any number of different nouns, but we don't know which one. If you're wondering who is knocking at your door and you aren't allowed to use the pronoun *who*, you'd have to start listing every noun you could think of. Is it Matt at my door? Is it Mom? Is it Santa? Is it the New York Giants? Is it Harry Potter? Is it . . . oh, my, how tired we would get if we couldn't use pronouns.

Watching out for crazy antecedents

A pronoun takes the place of a noun. The antecedent is the noun that the pronoun takes the place of or stands for.

Zack gave his sister her doll.
His is a pronoun. Who does it stand for? It stands for Zack, so the antecedent of *his* is *Zack*. The word *her* is also a pronoun and it stands for *sister*. The antecedent of *her* is *sister*.

If you put pronouns in odd places, it's hard to tell what the antecedent is, and sometimes sentences can get pretty crazy.

CRAZY:

It was pitch dark and my cat was still outdoors. I grabbed my flashlight to begin the search and listened for its purr.
The antecedent of *its* appears to be *flashlight*.

BETTER:

It was pitch dark and my cat was still outdoors. I grabbed my flashlight to begin the search and listened for Magic's purr.

CRAZY:

While driving it at 200 mph around the North Pole, Santa swerved to avoid hitting an elf and landed his sleigh in a snowdrift.

(The pronoun *it* appears early in this sentence, but we don't find out what *it* is until the end of the sentence—and by that time we have an elf and a snowdrift to deal with as well.)

BETTER:

While driving his sleigh at 200 mph around the North Pole, Santa swerved to avoid hitting an elf and landed in a snowdrift.

CRAZY:

Driving home late last night, a deer suddenly appeared in our headlights.

(What this means: A deer, driving home late last night, suddenly appeared in our headlights. We suspect that deer was driving without a license.)

BETTER:

Driving home last night, we suddenly saw a deer in our headlights.

When is Josh a "him" and when is he a "he"?

Which is correct?

I like you better than him.
I like you better than he.

Both are correct, but they mean entirely different things.

I like you better than him = I like you better than I like him.
I like you better than he = I like you better than he likes you.

Pronouns come in three groups called cases.

>*Subjective case*—the doer (subject) of the action:
>   I throw the ball.
>*Objective case*—the receiver (object) of the action:
>   Throw the ball to me.
>*Possessive case*—shows ownership:
>   My throw to third base won the game!

Subjective Case	Objective Case	Possessive Case
I sing.	Sing to me.	my song
You sing.	Joe sings to you.	your song
She sings.	Sing to her.	her song
He sings.	Sing to him.	his song
It sings.	Sing to it.	its song
We sing.	Sing to us.	our song
They sing.	Sing to them.	their song
Who sings?	To whom does Joe sing?	whose song

What is wrong with these sentences?

Mom cooked dinner for Archer and I.
Her and I went to the mall after school.
Us eighth graders are studying algebra.
She is taller than me.

Each of the underlined pronouns is wrong. How can you tell whether to use a subjective pronoun or an objective pronoun? Actually, it's very easy. Almost none of us grown-ups worry "oh, objective or subjective?" No, we just juggle words until the sentence sounds right. All you have to do is add words or delete words until you can tell which pronoun sounds right.

ADD WORDS:

Mom cooked dinner for Archer and (for) I. Sounds wrong.
Mom cooked dinner for Archer and (for) me. Much better.

RIGHT:

Mom cooked dinner for Archer and me.

ADD WORDS:

Her (went) and I went to the mall after school. Sounds wrong.
She (went) and I went to the mall after school. Much better.

RIGHT:

She and I went to the mall after school.

DELETE WORDS:

Us ~~eighth graders~~ are studying algebra. Sounds wrong.
We ~~eighth graders~~ are studying algebra. Much better.

RIGHT:

We eighth graders are studying algebra.

ADD WORDS:

She is taller than me (am tall). Sounds wrong.
She is taller than I (am tall). Much better.

RIGHT:

She is taller than I.

Here is another trick to use when you are confused: turn the sentence around and notice what sounds right.

WHICH IS RIGHT:

In language arts, the best students are Laney and (me/I).

TURN IT AROUND:

Me am the best student. Sounds wrong.
I am the best student. Much better.

RIGHT:

In language arts, the best students are Laney and I.

WHICH IS RIGHT:

The winner of the award for fastest pizza eater is (he/him).

TURN IT AROUND:

Him is the winner. Sounds wrong.
He is the winner. Much better.

RIGHT:

The winner of the award for fastest pizza eater is he.

Polite pronouns
It is considered polite to put yourself second.

WRONG:

Me and Finley want to play soccer.

RIGHT BUT NOT SO POLITE:

I and Finley want to play soccer.

POLITE:

Finley and I want to play soccer.

WRONG:

Mom gave the cookies to her and I.

RIGHT BUT NOT SO POLITE:

Mom gave the cookies to me and her.

POLITE:

Mom gave the cookies to her and me.

Is it me or is it I? It's a hot debate.

Is this right?	Or is this right?
It's me.	It's I.
It's him.	It's he.
It's her.	It's she.
It's us.	It's we.
It's them.	It's they.

Even the experts don't agree on this one. According to the strictest rules, *it's me* is wrong. (Turn the sentence around. You would never say "me am it." You would say "I am it.") However, *it's me* is so commonly used that it is gaining acceptance as an idiom (a commonly used phrase that might be peculiar, but is accepted as correct English). In informal speech and writing, *it's me* is okay. Even in more formal writing, *it's me* is often used and is not frowned on as much as *it's her* or *it's him*. In formal writing, even if you use *it's me*, still always use *it's she* and *it's he*.

The ubiquitous *you*

Ubiquitous means "it's everywhere! It's everywhere!" *You* is one of the most overused words in our language. In formal writing, be careful. When using the word *you*, the writer should really mean "you, the reader," not someone, anyone, or everyone.

INFORMAL:

If you add one and one, you get two.

FORMAL:

One plus one equals two.

INFORMAL:

You have to pay $9.50 to get into the movie.

FORMAL:

The movie costs $9.50.

INFORMAL:

If you're late for school, you'll get in trouble.

FORMAL:

Students who are late for school will get in trouble.

The capital *I*

Why is *I* the only capitalized pronoun? Is it because I am so important? The word *I* is not capitalized in Spanish, French, German, and many other languages. The answer is simple: A little tiny *i* all by itself looks like it's missing something, like other parts of the word fell off or got lost. So the little tiny *i* grew taller over the years and eventually turned into a capital letter.

 BRAIN TICKLERS Set # 2

Find the goofs in these sentences and correct them.

1. Jillian remembered to bring Lydia's jacket to school but forgot her gloves.

2. They don't allow kids to throw jello at each other in the cafeteria.

3. When doing a plié, the ballerina should keep her knees over her toes. You shouldn't allow your knees to turn inward or you could damage your knees and ankles.

4. I gave Charlie a new bike and a video game; it made him happy.

5. Hello. You want to speak to Esperanza? This is her.

6. We had a great time at Myrtle Beach; they have so much to do there.

7. The teacher told we kids to be quiet.

8. We're going out to dinner alone—just Gabriela and me.

9. It was him who ate all the nachos.

10. Mom gave both of us, Elizabeth and I, money for the movie.

11. Yuriko is a friend of Miranda's and me.

12. Don't tell anyone! Keep this a secret between you and I.

(Answers are on pages 54–55.)

Verb Pointers

What is a verb?

It is a word that shows action or state of being.

- action: run, swim, jump, leap, fall, dream
- state of being (something or someone is being described, but no action is going on): be, appear, seem, feel

I can make plenty of interesting sentences without nouns. For example:

Don't do that. It's dangerous, and if you do it enough, it could hurt you!
I like you, you like me, they like us—everybody's happy.
That's enough of this. Let's go outside and play!

Not bad, huh? Try to make a juicy sentence without a verb. Okay, sentence fragments maybe:

Wow! What a great bike.
Yum. Good food. More cookies anywhere?

But how long can you live on fragments? Try writing a real sentence without verbs.

There no way we without verbs. Nothing. Without any action words, our sentences . . . very dull. No communication. Action . . . being . . . without them, well, nothing.

We need verbs! Here are some ways to treat verbs with respect and to avoid the verb goofs students often make.

Verb tenses

Verb tenses let us know when the action happens.

Here are the six tenses you have to choose from:

Present tense: I *eat* pizza often.

Past tense: I *ate* pizza last night.

Future tense: I *will eat* pizza later today.

Present perfect tense: I *have eaten* pizza many times.

Past perfect tense: By the time you arrived, I *had eaten* the whole pizza.

Future perfect tense: I *will have eaten* pizza at least a million times by the year 2020.

Here are the six progressive forms (progressive means that the action continues for a while):

Present progressive: I *am eating* pizza.

Past progressive: I *was eating* pizza when you called.

Future progressive: I *will be eating* pizza at 8:30 tonight.

Present perfect progressive: I *have been eating* pizza all day.

Past perfect progressive: I *had been eating* pizza for three hours when Mom said my eyeballs looked like pepperonis.

Future perfect progressive: I *will have been eating* pizza for five hours nonstop when bedtime rolls around.

Here are the three uses of the emphatic form (which include the words *do, does,* or *did* with the verb):

Emphasis: I *do eat* pizza! When I was a kid, wow, *did* I *eat* pizza.

Questions: *Do* I *eat* pizza? *Did* I really *eat* 25 pizzas?

Negatives: I *do not eat* green, leafy vegetables—only pizza; however, I *did not eat* all 25 pizzas by myself. (In many other languages, the negative is formed by adding a "no." In Spanish, for example, we say "como" for "I eat" and "no como" for "I do not eat." This is a simple and easy way of creating a negative, but in English, we do not say "I no eat" or "I no sleep." We use the more complicated emphatic form instead.)

When to use the present tense:

Present action: I *want* to eat pizza right now.

Action that happens over and over: I *eat* pizza almost every day.

Scientific facts and other things that are always true: Eating 25 pizzas a day *is* not good for you.

Headlines: "Local Kid Nearly *Explodes* from Pizza Overdose"

Sometimes the present tense is used in place of the future tense: Tomorrow I *leave* for a special hospital to try to overcome my pizza addiction.

In book reports (stories often occur "in the present" as a reader reads them): In the final scenes of *Pizza Panic*, the hero of the story *is* cured of his pizza addiction and *lives* happily ever after, never again craving mozzarella and pepperoni.

Be consistent with tenses.

WEAK:

I got home late and Mom fusses at me for not calling to let her know where I will be.

> I got home = past tense
> Mom fusses = present tense
> where I will be = future tense

BETTER:

I got home late and Mom fussed at me for not calling to let her know where I
was.

    I got home = past tense
    Mom fussed = past tense
    where I was = past tense

WEAK:

My puppy had been eating his puppy chow for five minutes when the
doorbell rings and he is rushing through the house to see who's there, and
on the way to the door he bumped into the coffee table and breaks a coffee
cup that was there.

    puppy had been eating = past perfect progressive tense
    doorbell rings = present tense
    he is rushing = present progressive tense
    who's there = who is there = present tense
    he bumped = past tense
    breaks a coffee cup = present tense
    cup that was there = past tense

BETTER:

My puppy had been eating his puppy chow for five minutes when the
doorbell rang and he rushed through the house to see who was there, and
on the way to the door he bumped into the coffee table and broke a coffee
cup that was there.

    puppy had been eating = past perfect progressive tense
    doorbell rang = past tense
    he rushed = past tense
    who was there = past tense
    he bumped = past tense
    broke a coffee cup = past tense
    cup that was there = past tense

Is your voice active or passive?

Most writers and editors dislike the passive voice. They say it's too
blah.

PASSIVE VOICE:

The ball was hit.
(By whom? The passive voice hides the doer of the action.)

ACTIVE VOICE:

Zhen hit the ball.

PASSIVE VOICE:

My nose was punched by you.
(At least we know who did it, but nobody talks this way.)

ACTIVE VOICE:

You punched me in the nose!

You can see from these examples that the passive voice is less dynamic than the active voice because it ignores or downplays the doer of the action. Imagine you are a sportswriter for your school paper. Which voice do you think your readers would find more interesting?

PASSIVE VOICE:

The ball was hit and a run was scored. The score was kept and eventually the game was won. Strong emotions were felt by the fans and much applause was heard.

ACTIVE VOICE:

In the bottom of the ninth inning, James slammed the ball across the fence, and every player on the previously loaded bases came home. Our team won 10–8! The crowd went wild!

The passive voice is often better in these cases:

- The doer of the action is not important or not known.

PASSIVE VOICE:

School is canceled today!
(Who cares who canceled it?)

PASSIVE VOICE:

The water was contaminated.
(Nobody knows who or what contaminated it.)

- You want to be polite, avoid sounding bossy, or soften a strong statement.

PASSIVE VOICE:

Your application was rejected.

ACTIVE VOICE:

We rejected your application.

PASSIVE VOICE:

The test must be finished in one hour.

ACTIVE VOICE:

You must finish the test in one hour.

- You want to emphasize the thing you're talking about, not the person who does the action.

PASSIVE VOICE:

This big blue ribbon [emphasizing the thing] will be given to the winner.

ACTIVE VOICE:

The winner [emphasizing the person] will receive this big blue ribbon.

- You are writing in an impersonal, scientific manner.

PASSIVE VOICE:

The mice were separated into two groups.

ACTIVE VOICE:

My lab partner and I separated the mice into two groups.

Some tricky irregular verbs

Here is the format for the following examples:

Today I ___.   Yesterday I ___.   Many times I have ___.

Present   Past   Past Participle

Regular verbs work this way:

Today	Yesterday	Many times
cook	cooked	cooked
fix	fixed	fixed
pick	picked	picked
jump	jumped	jumped

Regular verbs are easy. Unfortunately, irregular verbs aren't so easy. Sometimes there's a pattern to irregular verbs.

Today	Yesterday	Many times
blow	blew	blown
grow	grew	grown
know	knew	known
throw	threw	thrown
sell	sold	sold
tell	told	told

Sometimes there's no pattern.

Today	Yesterday	Many times
ride	rode	ridden
slide	slid	slid
wake	woke	woken
take	took	taken
make	made	made
eat	ate	eaten
beat	beat	beaten

Sometimes when you think there's a pattern, along comes a surprise.

	Today	Yesterday	Many times
If it's	drink	drank	drunk
and it's	sink	sank	sunk
and it's	shrink	shrank	shrunk
why is it	think	thought	thought
If it's	sing	sang	sung
and it's	ring	rang	rung
and it's	spring	sprang	sprung
why is it	fling	flung	flung

TROUBLING VERBS

If you grew up speaking English, you know that we say "the teacher taught," but we don't say "the preacher praught." Your ear will tell you that it's fine to say that you "wrote your sister," but it's not fine to say that you "bote your sister" if what you did was bite her. You know most irregular verbs by ear, but here are a few troublemakers. (When two words are given, either is okay but the first choice is a little better.)

Bite, bit, bitten or bit
Bring, brought, brought—*brang* and *brung* are not words
Drag, dragged, dragged—*drug* is often used but not correct
Dive, dived or dove, dived

Drive, drove, driven—*drived* is not a word
Forget, forgot, forgotten or forgot
Get, got, gotten or got
Hang (to hang a picture or to dangle): hang, hung, hung
Hang (to hang a horse thief): hang, hanged, hanged
Hide, hid, hid or hidden
Kneel, knelt or kneeled, knelt or kneeled
Leap, leaped or leapt, leaped or leapt
Prove, proved, proved or proven
Rise, rose, risen—*rised* is not a word
Shine (to polish, as in to shine silver): shine, shined, shined
Shine (to give off light like a star): shine, shone, shone
Shrink, shrank or shrunk, shrunk or shrunken
Sing, sang, sung
Sink, sank, sunk—*sinked* is not a word
Spring, sprang or sprung, sprung
Stink, stank or stunk, stunk
Sweat, sweat or sweated, sweat or sweated
Swim, swam, swum
Swing, swung, swung
Tread, trod or treaded, trodden or trod
Wake, woke or waked, waked or woken

The most commonly used verb in the English language, and the most oddly irregular verb in the English language, is *to be*. How did *I am*, *you are*, *he is*, *I was*, and *you were* come from the word *be*? The verb *to be* is highly irregular in many other languages, too, largely because it is the most basic verb there is; therefore, it is very old in all languages, and it has evolved in some odd ways. Fortunately, most people use this verb correctly in English, so it doesn't cause students a lot of problems.

CAUTION—Major Mistake Territory!

Confusing *lie* and *lay* is probably the #1 mistake in the English language—and I do not lie!

Lie and lay

People lie on beds. Dogs lie on people. Fleas lie on dogs. The people, the dogs, and the fleas are very still. *Lie* is a still verb.

A person picks up a dog and lays it on a blanket. A pair of tweezers picks a flea off a dog and lays it outside. A hen lays an egg. The person, the tweezers, and the hen are very active. *Lay* is an active verb. Somebody or something is setting or placing something somewhere.

Chances are that over half the adults in the United States use these verbs wrong, and that includes many writers, teachers, and high-powered public speakers. Why are these two verbs such troublemakers? It's not because they are spelled similarly. We don't mix up the verbs *put* and *pat*, or the verbs *shop* and *ship*. So that can't be the reason. It's partly because we hear them used wrong so often that our ears tell us that wrong is normal. Does "lay down on the floor" sound okay to you? If it does, your poor ears have been corrupted!

Another reason these verbs are so hard to get right is that the verb *to lie* is an oddly irregular verb that actually uses the word *lay* in its conjugation. Let's see how that works:

Today I lie on the sofa.
Yesterday I lay on the sofa.
Many times I have lain on the sofa.

Yet another reason these verbs are tricky is that they often go hand-in-hand.

I lay my beach towel on the sand, then I lie down on it.
Mom lays the groceries on the kitchen counter, but then those lazy groceries just lie there until she puts them away.

Let's see how these tricky verbs work.

Lie (to lie down on a bed): lie, lay, lain, lying

Today I lie in bed.
Yesterday I lay in bed.
Many times I have lain in bed.
Yesterday I was lying in bed all day.
Lying in bed all day is boring.

Lay (to place something, to set something down): lay, laid, laid, laying

Today I lay the book on the counter.
Yesterday I laid the book on the counter.
Many times I have laid the book on the counter.
Yesterday I was laying the book on the counter when Mom came home.
Laying books on the kitchen counter is against the rules in my house.

Here are some tips for remembering these very important and very tricky verbs:

- It may be helpful to repeat this to yourself like a little song: lie, lay, lain, lie, lay, lain. It's sort of like the "*i* before *e* except after *c* . . ." song that helps us remember spelling rules. If you get stuck on that odd verb *to lie*, start through this little ditty and you'll quickly find the right word.

- Remember that the verb *to lay* is really not very odd. It works just like *to say* and *to pay*. Those verbs are irregular, but they aren't confusing. Today I say that I pay; yesterday I said that I paid; many times I have said that I have paid. *To lay* works the same way: lay, laid, laid.

- Nobody says that hens lie eggs. We all get that one correct: hens *lay* eggs. And those hens are mighty busy! Visualize how active and busy those hens are laying one egg after another. *Lay* is an active, busy word. When you're doing something active (laying down your backpack, laying a new rug on the floor), *lay* is the word you want.

- Remember that *lie* is a quiet word. Here's a silly ditty you can use to remind yourself of that (notice all the "eye" sounds): At night, I turn out my light and lie. Whether it's on your sofa, on your beach towel, or on your bed, if you are quietly reclining, you're lying—never laying.

- Substitute the word *put*. If the sentence sounds right, *lay* is the word you want. If it doesn't sound right, *lie* is the word you want. Does it sound right to say that you *put* the book on the table? Yes, so it's correct to say that you *lay* the book on the table. Does it sound right to say that your dog is *putting* on the floor? No, so it is correct to say that your dog is *lying* on the floor.

Lie (to tell a fib): lie, lied, lied, lying

RIGHT:

I think he's lying. He told the police he had been lying in bed all night near his buddy, who lay on the couch. Meanwhile, the bag of coins lay in the straw near the hens laying eggs in the coop. I'm sure he's lied many times about where he's lain after laying the stolen money in some sneaky place. What a lying liar!

What mood is your verb in?

Verb moods indicate the attitude of the speaker. Verbs have several different moods.

The **indicative mood** is by far the most common. The speaker is stating a fact or describing something. Most of our sentences are indicative.

A pizzly bear is a cross between a polar bear and a grizzly bear.
I have a pet pizzly bear. As pets go, he is quite huge.

The **imperative mood** makes a command.

Get that pizzly bear out of my kitchen!
And don't let him back in here!

The **interrogative mood** asks a question.

Why is Mom so mean to my pizzly bear?
Doesn't she like him?

The **conditional mood** depends on something else to happen. If you see the words *could*, *would*, or *might*, it is likely that the sentence is in the conditional mood.

My pizzly bear might bite you if you step on his foot.
My pizzly bear would be able to sleep in my bed if he weighed a few hundred pounds less than he does.

In the **subjunctive mood**, the speaker is expressing ideas that are actually not true—perhaps a wish, a desire, or an imaginary situation.

WRONG:

I were born in 1999.

RIGHT:

I was born in 1999.

This is obvious, right? Sure it is—at least most of the time. Sometimes, however, we do say "if I were" or "if she were." This is the subjunctive mood, and it indicates to the reader that the writer is saying "this is not actual fact." I think of subjunctive statements as "what if" and "if only" ideas.

IF ONLY:

If I <u>were</u> a magician, I would turn the entire world into chocolate.

WHAT IF:

If <u>she</u> <u>were</u> to win the $10 million lottery, how do you think she would spend the money?

IF ONLY:

If <u>I</u> <u>were</u> an eagle, I would soar high above mountains and deep into canyons. I have wished many times that <u>I</u> <u>were</u> an eagle.

WHAT IF:

If <u>you</u> <u>were</u> a dolphin, do you think you would prefer fish or seaweed for dinner?

BACK TO REALITY:

I think <u>I</u> <u>was</u> 17 when we moved to our new house. But if <u>I</u> <u>was</u> 16 when we moved, then the year would have been 1995.
(This is a statement of fact, not *what if*.)

The subjunctive is also used for suggestions, commands, urgency, and recommendations.

STATEMENT:

School <u>is</u> canceled.

SUGGESTION:

I politely suggest that school <u>be</u> canceled forever.

STATEMENT:

Darnell <u>eats</u> all ten bagels.

COMMAND:

I command that Darnell <u>eat</u> all ten bagels that he ordered.

STATEMENT:

Juan <u>gives</u> his homework attention.

URGENCY:

It is essential that Juan <u>give</u> his homework more attention.

STATEMENT:

We <u>are</u> finished with subjunctives.

RECOMMENDATION:

I vote that we <u>be</u> finished with subjunctives.

When is a verb not a verb?

There are three ways we create words from verbs, words that then play an entirely different role in the sentence. It's sort of like putting wings on a car and turning it into an airplane. What started out as a car is now operating as something quite different. These not-real-verbs made from verbs are called verbals. How about that for a clever name! Let's see what they look like and how they work.

Infinitives

Add the word *to* in front of a verb and you have an infinitive: to sing, to dance, to leap, to sleep. They look like verbs and sound like verbs, but they never play the role of a verb in a sentence. What roles do infinitives play? An infinitive is often the subject of a sentence: To eat watermelon on a hot summer day is divine. (See page 62 for more information on what a subject is.) However, they can show up in lots of different ways. Here are a few examples:

I want to leap tall buildings with a single bound.
The class to ace is English.
I said that just to be silly.

To split or not to split? Many teachers will tell you never to split an infinitive. This is an old rule that some teachers think is still important and other teachers say is outdated. Here's what splitting infinitives looks like:

Infinitive	Non-split infinitive	Split infinitive
to run	to run quickly	to quickly run
to swim	to swim eagerly	to eagerly swim
to jump	to jump suddenly	to suddenly jump

WEAK:

It is usually better to not split infinitives.

BETTER:

It is usually better not to split infinitives.

It is okay to split an infinitive when you want to emphasize the word or words in between.

RIGHT:

I want you to study the material for the test.

MORE EMPHASIS:

I want you <u>to</u> thoroughly <u>study</u> the material for the test.

When you split an infinitive, be careful not to put too many words between *to* and the verb.

CONFUSING:

I want you <u>to</u> thoroughly and deliberately, without cutting any corners or making any excuses, <u>study</u> for the test.

BETTER:

I want you <u>to</u> thoroughly and deliberately <u>study</u> for the test without cutting any corners or making any excuses.

Gerunds

Add *-ing* to the end of a verb and you have a gerund. This is our second type of verbal. Gerunds can play any role in a sentence that a noun can play. Here are some examples:

I run [verb]. <u>Running</u> [gerund, noun, and subject of the sentence] is fun.

<u>Swimming</u> a mile [gerund phrase, subject of the sentence] is a lot harder than running a mile.

After <u>swimming</u> a mile [object of the preposition *after*], I was more than exhausted.

Gerunds are nouns, and what applies to nouns applies to gerunds. We don't say "me house," we say "my house." So it is almost always correct to say "my running" instead of "me running" and "my singing" instead of "me singing."

WRONG:

Mom doesn't like me eating too much ice cream.

RIGHT:

Mom doesn't like my eating too much ice cream.

WRONG:

Marianne feeding her kitty from her baby bottle is really cute.

RIGHT:

Marianne's feeding her kitty from her baby bottle is really cute.

If the emphasis is on the action, always use the possessive case.

(See page 14 for more on the possessive case.)

I hope you don't mind my eating the last apple.

But if you want to strongly emphasize the doer of the action, you have the option of using the objective case.

(See page 14 for more on the objective case.)

I hope you don't mind me holding your hand. (I'm glad it's just *me* holding your hand—not the other girls!)

Participles

This is our third type of verbal. Let's see what participles look like:

The verb	The present participle	The past participle
freeze	my freezing fingers	my frozen fingers
break	the breaking news	his broken arm
boil	the boiling egg	the boiled egg

One of the main jobs of participles is to function as adjectives, describing nouns. (See page 34 for more about adjectives.)

The soccer players, <u>exhausted</u> and <u>starving</u>, were happy when the match was finally over.
(*Exhaust* and *starve* are both verbs. *Exhausted* is a past participle, *starving* is a present participle, and both are adjectives describing the soccer players.)

The <u>crying</u> child, <u>frightened</u> by the large dog, ran to her mother.
(*Cry* and *frighten* are both verbs. *Crying* is a present participle, *frightened* is a past participle, and both are adjectives describing the little girl.)

Just for fun

If this is right	today he speaks, yesterday he spoke
Then why don't we say	the faucet leaks, yesterday it loke
If this is right	today I do, yesterday I did
Then why don't we say	today cows moo, yesterday they mid
And	today I boo-hoo, yesterday I bid-hid
If this is right	today I see, yesterday I saw
Then why don't we say	today I flee, yesterday I flaw
And	today I agree, yesterday I agraw
And	today I guarantee, yesterday I guarantaw
If this is right	you strike the ball, yesterday you struck it
Then why don't we say	you hike the ball, yesterday you huck it
And	you like the pie, yesterday you luck it
If this is right	today I think, yesterday I thought
Then why don't we say	today I sink, yesterday I sought

If this is right	today you fly, yesterday you flew
Then why don't we say	today you cry, yesterday you crew
If this is right	today I freeze, yesterday I froze
Then why don't we say	today I sneeze, yesterday I snoze
If this is right	today I sit, yesterday I sat
Then why don't we say	the dress doesn't fit, but yesterday it fat

BRAIN TICKLERS   Set # 3

Find the goofs in these sentences and correct them.

1. Mom fusses a lot about me trashing my room.

2. When I was a kid, I swang every day on an old tire my dad hanged in a tree for me.

3. I wish I'd waken up earlier.

4. Bill breaks the dish when he tossed it to Laura who is standing at the sink.

5. If I was you, I'd buy that gorgeous dress.

6. I've laid awake all night worrying about my math test.

7. I worked for three hours, and finally the assignment was completed.

8. I'm sure I lay my assignment on the teacher's desk yesterday. Where could it possibly have gone?

9. If you want to really, truly, without a doubt thrill your teacher, don't split infinitives.

10. The headline read "Local Kid Won Scholarship from Pizza Hut."

11. Brinley is dressed up today like she was Princess of Everywhere.

12. The scientist insisted that dinosaurs were extinct.

13. Davis throwing a spit wad at Joe made Joe mad.

(Answers are on pages 55–57.)

Adjective and Adverb Pointers

What is an adjective?

It is a word that describes a noun or a pronoun and tells these things:

- which one: this, that, these
- what kind: red, large, sick, cloudy, enormous, petite
- how many: six, four hundred, many, several

What is an adverb?

It is a word that describes a verb, an adjective, or another adverb (not a noun) and tells these things:

- where: there, here, outside, inside, away
- when: now, then, later, immediately, yesterday
- how: quickly, slowly, stupidly, gracefully, effortlessly
- how often or how long: frequently, never, twice, sometimes
- how much: hardly, extremely, minimally, greatly, too, more

Adjectives with an -*ly* tail

Most adverbs are formed by adding -*ly* to the adjective, so if you see an -*ly* word, it's usually an adverb.

Adjective	Adverb
sad	sadly
slow	slowly
quick	quickly
tender	tenderly
artistic	artistically (notice the irregular spelling: -*ally*)
noisy	noisily (notice the irregular spelling: *y* becomes *i*)

What's the big deal?

Most of the time we automatically use adverbs and adjectives correctly. In these sentences, which is correct?

This is a (large/largely) house.
I am (extreme/extremely) tired.
He looked (stupid/stupidly) in that outfit.

No problem—right? Well, sometimes it's not so easy. Check this out:

WRONG:

This sentence is written awful bad.
(How is this sentence written? The question *how* implies that an adverb is needed, but *bad* is an adjective. *Badly* is an adverb.)

STILL WRONG:

This sentence is written awful badly.
(How badly? *How* implies that another adverb is needed, but *awful* is an adjective.)

RIGHT:

This sentence is not written awfully badly—it's perfect!

You can get away with a lot of goofs in everyday speech, but when you are writing a paper or giving a speech, adverb and adjective goofs make your work look sloppy. Can you see what's wrong with each of these sentences?

Samantha looks real good in her new dress.
Edward turned the corner too quick and crashed his bike.
I made an A on the exam so easy that my mom thinks I cheated.
Sammy and C.J. played awesome in the tennis match.
I want to get my driver's license so bad I could scream.

If you can't see what's wrong with these sentences, read on. Soon you will.

Some very common adjective and adverb goofs

Adjective	Adverb
bad	badly
real	really
sure	surely
easy	easily
good	well

In the following examples, <u>adjectives</u> are underlined and *adverbs* are italic.

WRONG:

I am real sure that this is a real diamond, not a fake.
(How sure? This question implies an adverb is needed: I am *really* sure.

What kind of diamond? This question implies an adjective is needed: a *real* diamond.)

RIGHT:

I am *really* sure that this is a <u>real</u> diamond, not a fake.

WRONG:

I did good on the exam and got a good grade on my report card.
(How did I do? An adverb is needed: I did *well*.
What kind of grade? An adjective is needed: a *good* grade.)

RIGHT:

I did *well* on the exam and got a <u>good</u> grade on my report card.

WRONG:

It was an easy match, and James won easy.
(What kind of match? An adjective is needed: an *easy* match.
How did he win? An adverb is needed: he won *easily*.)

RIGHT:

It was an <u>easy</u> match, and James won *easily*.

WRONG:

This sure seems like a sure bet.
(How does it seem? An adverb is needed: it *surely* seems.
What kind of bet? An adjective is needed: a *sure* bet.)

RIGHT:

This *surely* seems like a <u>sure</u> bet.

WRONG:

Only the bad ice skaters performed bad.
(What kind of ice skaters? An adjective is needed: *bad* ice skaters.
How did they perform? An adverb is needed: they performed *badly*.)

RIGHT:

Only the <u>bad</u> ice skaters performed *badly*.

Same word, different job
A few words can be either adjectives or adverbs depending on how they are used.

Adjective telling what kind	Adverb telling how, when, or where
He played a <u>hard</u> guitar piece.	He pounded the drums *hard*.
I flew past a <u>high</u> building.	I flew *high* in the sky.

We are <u>close</u> friends.   Sit *close* to me.

You're doing a <u>fine</u> job.   You are skiing *fine* since your lesson.

That was a <u>low</u> blow.   I stooped *low*.

She was in a <u>deep</u> sleep.   She dived *deep* into the water.

He is a <u>fair</u> player.   He's not cheating; he's playing *fair*.

I'm in a <u>tight</u> spot.   Sleep *tight*.

That's the <u>right</u> answer.   The teacher said I spelled it *right*.

That's the <u>wrong</u> answer.   The teacher said I spelled it *wrong*.

The <u>late</u> train arrives at 10:00.   I slept *late* this morning.

Draw a <u>straight</u> line.   Go *straight* to your room.

This is a <u>short</u> book.   I stopped *short* of finishing it.

You are on the <u>right</u> path.   Turn *right* at the next fork.

To make things even more complicated, most of these adverbs have two different forms: an *-ly* form and a form without the *-ly*. Notice that sometimes these two forms have very different meanings.

Adverb without *ly*	Adverb with *ly*
Billy hit Justin *hard*.	Billy *hardly* hit Justin.
Hold your head *high*.	I *highly* recommend it.
Becca and Emily sit *close* together.	The girls are *closely* related.
You are cooking dinner *fine*.	We need some *finely* chopped celery.
He dug *deep* into the earth.	He felt *deeply* happy.
He's playing *fair*.	He's playing *fairly* well.
Pull the ropes *tight*.	These ropes are *tightly* twisted.
The teacher said I spelled it *right*.	She praised me *rightly*.
The teacher said I spelled it *wrong*.	She accused me *wrongly*.
I've been sleeping *late*.	I haven't been sleeping *lately*.

Some adverbs don't have an *-ly* form.

Elias ran *fast*. It was a <u>fast</u> race. (*Fastly* is not a word.)
It won't be a <u>long</u> trip. I won't be gone *long*. (*Longly* is not a word.)
Austin got up *early* because he had an <u>early</u> class. (*Earlyly* is not a word.)

Some *-ly* words are adjectives. Here are a few:

friendly dog	lovely sunset	deadly chemicals
lowly job	hilly landscape	cowardly deed
early flight	oily rag	hourly chore

You can't always recognize an adverb by its *-ly* tail. You can recognize it by its job in the sentence: it tells you something about a verb, an adjective, or another adverb, never about a noun. And it answers one of these questions: *where? when? how? how often? how long?* or *how much?*

> ## REMINDER
>
> In this section <u>adjectives</u> are underlined and *adverbs* are italic.

Use adverbs with action verbs and adjectives with linking verbs.

Examples of action verbs: swim, run, jump, scream, write, sleep, eat, kiss, sit, cry, kick

She skates [action] *gracefully*.   He sings [action] *well*.
He leaves [action] *quickly*.   She yells [action] *loudly*.

The most common linking verb is *be* and all of its forms: *am, was, will be, have been, will have been,* etc. Notice that in these sentences the subject is being described but isn't actually doing any type of action.

Tori is [linking] <u>pretty</u>.   David was [linking] <u>thirsty</u>.
Erin and Avery are   Kacey and Tucker will be
   [linking] <u>tall</u>.   [linking] <u>hungry</u>.

Some words can be either linking verbs or action verbs depending on how they are used.

taste	sound	smell	feel	get
look	turn	grow	appear	act

Chris appears [linking—the subject is being described] <u>happy</u>.
The airplane appears [action] *suddenly* out of the fog.

Marcella feels [linking—the subject is being described] <u>tired</u>.
The vet feels [action] the cat's tummy *carefully*.

A trick to tell whether the verb is action or linking (in other words, whether to use an adjective or an adverb) is to substitute the word *seems* and notice how it sounds. If it sounds okay, it's a linking verb and you need an adjective. Otherwise, it's an action verb and you need an adverb.

The hamburger meat smells (bad/badly).

(The meat *seems* bad? Yes, that's okay, so *smell* here is a linking verb and needs an adjective. *Bad* is an adjective.)

I smelled the hamburger meat (careful/carefully) to see if it had gone bad.

(I *seem* the meat? No, that's not okay, so *smell* here is an action verb and needs an adverb. *Carefully* is an adverb.)

Comparisons: big–bigger–biggest
Big is called the positive; bigger is called the comparative; biggest is called the superlative.

For short adjectives and adverbs, add -*er* and -*est*.

Mary is thin, Lisa is thinner, Katie is thinnest.
Camilla is smart, Lavonda is smarter, Lindsey is smartest.
Come soon. Come sooner. Come the soonest you can.

For longer adjectives and most adverbs, use *more* and *most*.

ADJECTIVES:

I am capable. You are more capable. Catherine is most capable.

ADVERBS:

I eat quickly. You eat more quickly. She eats most quickly.

Or *less* and *least*.

ADJECTIVES:

Kristopher is willing. Eric is less willing. Of the three, Rick is least willing.

ADVERBS:

Branch runs gracefully. Sam runs less gracefully. Of the three, Mark runs least gracefully.

Sometimes you, the writer, must decide which sounds better, the *-er* form or the *more* form. Which do you think is better?

RIGHT:

Today is cloudier than the weather forecaster predicted.

RIGHT:

Today is more cloudy than the weather forecaster predicted.

RIGHT:

That donkey is even stupider than I thought.

RIGHT:

That donkey is even more stupid than I thought.

A few adverbs don't follow the rules. These are irregular:

You sing *well*. He sings *better*. Of the three, she sings *best*.
I ski *badly*. He skis *worse*. Of the three, she skis *worst*.
I ran *far*. You ran *farther*. Of the three, he ran *farthest*.

A few adjectives don't follow the rules. These are irregular:

Pete is a <u>good</u> athlete. Evan is a <u>better</u> athlete. Lucy is the <u>best</u> athlete.
Beets are <u>bad</u>. Olives are <u>worse</u>. Brussels sprouts are <u>worst</u>.
I have <u>little</u> luck. You have <u>less</u> luck. He has the <u>least</u> luck.
I have <u>many</u> cats. You have <u>more</u> cats. She has the <u>most</u> cats.
I ate too <u>much</u> pizza. He ate <u>more</u> pizza. You ate the <u>most</u> pizza.

Comparisons can get confusing. Try to keep them as simple as possible. Check these out:

Confusing	Clear
less big	smaller
more powerless	less powerful
least harmless	most harmful
less unable	more able

Some adjectives can't get any bigger or better—they are already superlative.

WRONG:

I am the onliest girl on the football team.

WRONG:

I am the most only girl on the football team.

RIGHT:

I am the only girl on the football team.

Here are some other adjectives that work this way: *first, best, unique, perfect, round, square, one-of-a-kind.*

Be careful where you place adverbs.

WEAK:

I had *only* been asleep for ten minutes when the phone rang and woke me up.
(This sentence actually means this: I had only been sleeping—I hadn't been jogging or eating or dancing—for ten minutes when the phone rang.)

BETTER:

I had been asleep for *only* ten minutes when the phone rang and woke me up.

NOT VERY ROMANTIC:

My darling, I *only* think about you.
(Does this mean you never *feel* anything about me?)

BETTER:

My darling, I think *only* about you.

 **BRAIN TICKLERS** Set # 4

Find the goofs in these sentences and correct them.

1. The dog smells badly.

2. Of the three boys, Will runs faster.

3. You sure can eat a lot of ice cream at one sitting!

4. This is a real pretty dress.

5. Apples turn badly if you let them sit out too long.

6. This bottle of milk is emptier than that one.

7. I only ate three slices of pizza.

8. What a nice gesture on your part to greet them so nice when they arrived.

9. Josh's mom hugged him real sweet and said, "Enough grammar exercises. Let's take a break."

(Answers are on pages 57–58.)

Conjunction Pointers

What is a conjunction?

It is a word that joins words or groups of words.

Life without conjunctions:

I would love to go out to eat with you. I would love to go out to eat with Lela. I would love to go to the movie with you. I would love to go to the movie with Lela. My mom says I can't. My mom says I might have to do my homework. My mom says I might have to clean up my room. The reason is this: I broke my curfew last weekend.

Life with conjunctions:

I would love to go out to eat <u>and</u> to the movie with you <u>and</u> Lela, <u>but</u> my mom says I have to <u>either</u> do my homework <u>or</u> clean up my room <u>because</u> I broke my curfew last weekend.

There are three types of conjunctions, each with a fancy and confusing name: coordinating conjunctions, subordinate conjunctions, and correlative conjunctions. I wish they had just been named Conjunction 1, Conjunction 2, and Conjunction 3. Should we write our governors and congresspeople and try to get these names changed?

Coordinating conjunctions

Coordinating conjunctions join two independent clauses—two separate, complete sentences, both of which make complete sense on their own.

We gave the dog a bath, <u>but</u> he jumped right back into the mud. ("We gave the dog a bath" is a complete sentence and makes sense all by itself. "He jumped right back into the mud" is a complete sentence and makes sense all by itself.)

He promised he would be a good dog, <u>yet</u> he was quite a bad dog. (Both of these are complete sentences and make sense by themselves.)

Coordinating conjunctions also join two words or two ideas that are grammatically similar, and they give equal emphasis to both words or ideas.

Join two nouns: I love potatoes <u>and</u> tomatoes.
Join two verbs: The child is kicking <u>and</u> screaming.
Join two adjectives: I want a red <u>or</u> yellow dress.
Join two adverbs: Run quickly <u>but</u> carefully.

There are only seven coordinating conjunctions and they are fairly easy to remember. They are all tiny little words, not one of them has more than three letters, and they spell out the acronym FANBOYS. Here is the entire list of coordinating conjunctions: *for, and, nor, but, or, yet, so.*

As a rule, don't begin a sentence with a coordinating conjunction.

WEAK:

I studied for the math test. But I didn't study enough.

BETTER:

I studied for the math test, but I didn't study enough.

WEAK:

I want to be a doctor when I grow up. Or maybe a tiger tamer.

BETTER:

I want to be a doctor when I grow up, or maybe a tiger tamer.

If you don't do it very often, sometimes beginning a sentence with a conjunction creates effective emphasis.

Orlando thought the noise he heard was a grizzly bear in his bedroom. And he was right!

Subordinate conjunctions

These conjunctions link a dependent clause to an independent clause (see page 63 for more information about these clauses). In short, an independent clause makes sense all by itself and can stand alone as a sentence. A dependent clause depends on the rest of the sentence to make sense; without the rest of the sentence, we don't have a clue what is happening.

I can't try out for the tennis team <u>because</u> I broke my foot last month. ("I can't try out for the tennis team." This makes sense all by itself. "Because I broke my foot last month." What? I don't understand. This is dependent on the rest of the sentence to make sense. That's why we call it a dependent clause.)

<u>While</u> I was riding my bike to school, both of my tires suddenly went flat. ("Both of my tires suddenly went flat" makes sense all by itself. "While I was riding my bike to school" is dependent on the rest of the sentence to make sense.)

Both of my tires suddenly went flat <u>while</u> I was riding my bike to school. (Notice that the subordinate conjunction can come at the beginning of the sentence or it can come later in the sentence. Both are correct.)

There are only a few coordinating conjunctions, but there is a whole slew of subordinate ones. Notice that when these conjunctions join clauses they tell us something about how the two clauses are related to each other. Here are some of the most commonly used subordinate conjunctions.

after	every time	so that
although	except	that
as	if	though
as if	in case	unless
as much as	in order that	until
as soon as	lest	when
as though	now that	whenever
because	once	where
before	only if	whereas
by the time	provided that	whether
even if	rather than	whether or not
even though	since	while

Some of these conjunctions can work as other parts of speech; for example, *once* can be an adverb (I once saw an eagle) and *until* can be a preposition (until lunch time). Just ask if a word or phrase is joining something. Is it joining two ideas, two clauses? If so, it is doing a conjunction's job.

Although we rarely begin a sentence with a coordinating conjunction (see page 43), we frequently begin sentences with subordinate conjunctions.

<u>Although</u> Davis is not afraid of rhinos, he knew his parents would not be happy with this scene.
<u>When</u> everybody else was fast asleep, he snuck the rhino out the back door.

Correlative conjunctions
These conjunctions are used in pairs.

either—or   neither—nor
not only—but also   both—and

WRONG:

Neither Wesley or Elizabeth got a hit in the game.

RIGHT:

Neither Wesley nor Elizabeth got a hit in the game.

WRONG:

Not only Maya but Ruth got a part in the play.

RIGHT:

Not only Maya but also Ruth got a part in the play.

ALSO RIGHT:

Both Maya and Ruth got a part in the play.

WRONG:

Sal cannot pitch nor catch.

RIGHT:

Sal can neither pitch nor catch.

ALSO RIGHT:

Sal cannot pitch or catch.

Comma caution

Avoid a common goof: don't use a comma every time you see a conjunction.

- Don't use a comma when you have a compound verb (a verb that has two or more parts).

WRONG:

Lily ate a big dinner, and slept soundly all night.
(The subject is *Lily*; the compound verb is *ate and slept*. You wouldn't write "Lily ate, and slept." Who needs the comma?)

RIGHT:

Lily ate a big dinner and slept soundly all night.

- Don't use a comma before subordinate conjunctions. Delete the comma in each of these sentences:

WRONG:

I will walk home, because my bicycle has two flat tires.

WRONG:

I will eat my spinach, if you'll put some butter on it.

WRONG:

I try to hide, whenever my mom serves liver for dinner.

- Don't use a comma before *and* when only two things are listed. Delete the comma in each of these sentences:

I love chocolate cake, and chocolate ice cream.
I want to play pro baseball, and pro football.

- When should you use commas with conjunctions? See pages 80–82.

Too many *and*'s

Don't overuse the conjunction *and*.

RIGHT BUT BORING:

I got up early, and I finished studying. I went to school, and I took the algebra quiz. I did well, and I felt relieved. I told my dad, and he was proud of me.

MUCH BETTER:

I got up early and finished studying for the algebra quiz before I went to school. I was relieved, and my dad was very proud that I did well on the quiz.

There are many ways to avoid the dull, boring pattern of too many *and*'s. This is just one way. Can you think of others?

Too many *so*'s

Don't overuse the conjunction *so*.

WEAK:

Thomas studied hard, so he got a good grade.

BETTER:

Thomas got a good grade because he studied hard.

WEAK:

The doll was old and torn, so I threw it away.

BETTER:

I threw away the old, torn doll.

Preposition Pointers
What is a preposition?

A preposition is a word that is always used with a noun or a pronoun to create what's called a prepositional phrase (for example, <u>in</u> the house, <u>on</u> the bike, <u>under</u> the water). The prepositional phrase shows a relationship (often a *position*) between that noun or pronoun and another word in the sentence.

In the house is a prepositional phrase. The preposition is the word *in* and the noun (which is called the object of the preposition) is the word *house*. Who or what is in the house? Let's say that Holly is in the house. The prepositional phrase shows a relationship between Holly and the house; it tells us where Holly is in relationship to the house. She is not under the house, she is not over the house, she is not beside the house, and she is not behind the house. She is in the house.

Here are some prepositions. Notice as you read these words that they all promise to tell us something about where something is, when something happens, or to show some other type of relationship between two things:

about	down	since
above	for	through
after	from	throughout
around	in	to
at	inside	underneath
before	of	up
beneath	off	with
between	on	without
by	opposite	

Check out what a big difference a little preposition can make:

I am swimming <u>toward</u> the shark's tummy. Oops.
I am swimming away <u>from</u> the shark's tummy as fast as I can. Hurry!
I am swimming <u>inside</u> the shark's tummy. Bummer.

Prepositions and their objects

A prepositional phrase has a preposition and an object of the preposition. The object can be a noun or a pronoun.

I am jumping <u>on</u> [preposition] the <u>trampoline</u> [noun/object].
I am swimming <u>in</u> [preposition] the very chilly <u>pond</u> [noun/object].
Julie is giving the gift <u>to</u> [preposition] <u>me</u> [pronoun/object].
Let's not leave <u>without</u> [preposition] <u>her</u> [pronoun/object] or <u>him</u> [pronoun/object].

If a prepositional phrase includes a pronoun, that pronoun must be in the objective case. (After all, it's the *object* of the preposition.) With nouns, there is no problem, as the noun doesn't change its form. Let's see how that works:

WHICH IS CORRECT:

The girl [subject] is hungry.
Give the pizza to [preposition] the girl [object].

Both are correct. You can see that the noun does not change based on how it is used in the sentence—in other words, it's the same whether it is subjective case or objective case. (See page 14 for more about cases.)

However, most pronouns do change.

WHICH IS CORRECT:

I [subject] am hungry. Give the pizza to [preposition] I [object].
I am hungry. Give the pizza to [preposition] me [object].

The latter pair of sentences is correct. "I" is subjective case so it works great when "I" is the subject of the sentence. "Me" is objective case, and "me" is the word you want when you have a prepositional phrase.

As a reminder, these are the objective case pronouns: me, you, him, her, it, whom, us, them. All of them change when they go from subjective case to objective case except for "it" and "you." These two pronouns stay the same. Check these out:

<u>It</u> is very clear; we need to learn a lesson from <u>it</u>.

("It" is the same whether it is the subject of the sentence or the object of a preposition.)

You know that I gave my last apple to you?
("You" is the same whether it is the subject of the sentence or the object of a preposition.)

Ending a sentence

It used to be a rigid rule that you should never end a sentence with a preposition. That rule has softened a lot over time. If you can change the order of the words so as not to end with a preposition and the sentence sounds good, do it, but if editing makes your sentence sound weird, forget it.

OKAY:

Notice the ease Hartley hits the ball with.

MORE FORMAL:

Notice the ease with which Hartley hits the ball.

OKAY:

A senator is someone most people look up to.

VERY WEIRD:

A senator is someone to whom most people upwardly look.

MUCH BETTER:

Most people look up to a senator.

RIGHT:

What time should we wake up?
(In this sentence, *up* is actually not a preposition; it's part of the verb *to wake up*. Here are some other "two-word" verbs that sound as if they end in a preposition: to sleep over, to lie down, to throw up, to shut down, to shut up, to shut out, to burn up, to burn down.)

Too much of a good thing
Don't use a bunch of prepositional phrases in a row.

AWKWARD:

I went to a store in a town in Ohio in the middle of a flood in June, which is during Ohio's rainy season, and in a matter of minutes found myself knee-deep in water.

Did you count all ten prepositional phrases? In each phrase, the preposition is underlined:

<u>to</u> a store   <u>in</u> a town   <u>in</u> Ohio
<u>in</u> the middle   <u>of</u> a flood   <u>in</u> June
<u>during</u> Ohio's rainy season   <u>in</u> a matter
<u>of</u> minutes   <u>in</u> water

BETTER:

Last June I visited a small Ohio town during the rainy season. When I went into a flooded store, I quickly found myself knee-deep in water.

Now we're down to only three prepositional phrases:

<u>during</u> the rainy season
<u>into</u> a flooded store
<u>in</u> water

When is a preposition not a preposition?

Remember that a word that looks like a preposition is playing that role in a sentence only if it is part of a prepositional phrase. Sometimes words we think of as prepositions are playing different roles.

PREPOSITIONS:

I went <u>up</u> the street, <u>down</u> the street, and <u>around</u> the corner.

ADVERBS:

Jump <u>up</u>, jump <u>down</u>, and turn <u>around</u>. (Jump where? Turn where? The question *where* usually implies that an adverb is needed.)

PREPOSITION:

Keep your hand <u>off</u> the off button.

ADJECTIVE:

Keep your hand off the <u>off</u> button. (What kind of button? That's a job for an adjective.)

PREPOSITION:

Climb <u>up</u> the ladder.

VERB:

Stand <u>up</u> for yourself. (*Stand up* is a two-word verb.)

PREPOSITION:

My house is just <u>before</u> the school.

CONJUNCTION:
Wash your hands <u>before</u> you eat.

Interjection Pointers
What is an interjection?
It is a little word that does these things:

- expresses a feeling: wow, gee, golly, oops, zowie, darn
- says yes or no: yes, no, yep, nope, uh-huh, uh-uh
- calls attention: yo, hey, whoa
- indicates a pause: well, um, hmm, ah

Standing alone
If an interjection expresses a really strong feeling, it can stand alone even though it's not a complete sentence. (What is a complete sentence? See page 62.) These sentence fragments are okay:

<u>Wow</u>! That's the coolest bike I've ever seen.
<u>Ouch</u>! That hurts.

BRAIN TICKLERS   Set # 5

Find the goofs in these sentences and correct them.

1. I want new rollerblades. And I want a new game for the computer for my birthday.

2. Jamie ate a plate of spaghetti, and a salad.

3. Hannah got dressed and headed out for her horseback lesson and got there early and she groomed her horse slowly.

4. Neither Eli or Brian was able to go with us to the game.

5. Oh, thank you, Dad! This is exactly the birthday present I was hoping for!

6. We drove in our new car in a hard rain through an open field over an old bridge to the house in the country where my grandmother lives.

7. Whoa, slow down, Princess, you're galloping too fast!

(Answers are on pages 59–60.)

BRAIN TICKLERS—THE ANSWERS
Set # 1, page 11

1. Lucas' house is next door to Bill Gates' house; I bet he gets a lot of hand-me-down computers!

   When a proper noun ends in an *s*, the modern style is to add an apostrophe and another *s* to show possession. The old-fashioned style was simply to add an apostrophe and no extra *s*. You could certainly argue that this sentence is correct as it is. However, if we were speaking this sentence, most of us would say *Lucas-es house*, so it would probably be best to write that as *Lucas's house*. Would we say *Bill Gates-es house*? Some people would and some people wouldn't. You wouldn't be wrong to spell this either way: *Bill Gates' house* or *Bill Gates's house*.

2. Lily is captain of the girl's softball team.

   Girl's is singular, so this sentence actually means that there is only one girl on the team. I bet you mean this: Lily is captain of the girls' softball team.

3. The womans' dress is made of silk.

   Womans' is not a word. Both of these are correct:

   • The <u>woman's</u> dress is made of silk.
   • The <u>women's</u> dresses are made of silk.

4. Marshall and David's fingers were nearly frostbitten after playing in the snow for three hours.

   Marshall and David's fingers implies that Marshall and David share a set of fingers. It could also imply that Marshall's whole body was nearly frostbitten and David's fingers were nearly frostbitten. This is correct: <u>Marshall's</u> and <u>David's</u> fingers were nearly frostbitten after playing in the snow for three hours.

5. I asked dad to drive me to Maryanne's house.

   Capitalize *Father* or *Dad* when you're calling his name or referring to him without the word *my*. Both of these are correct:

   • I asked my dad to drive me to Maryanne's house.
   • I asked Dad to drive me to Maryanne's house.

6. The Earth is home to dozens of species of Monkeys, more types of Fungi and Mushrooms than we can count, and many fascinating creatures living deep in the Ocean that we have yet to discover.

   This sentence fell hard into the Cap Trap! There is actually only one word in this sentence that should be capitalized, and it's the first word of the sentence. I try to go very light on caps, making myself justify every single word that gets a capital letter to ensure that I won't overuse them.

7. I heard the babie's cries.

   Babie's is not a word.

   - If you mean one baby making one sound: I heard the <u>baby's cry</u>.
   - If you mean one baby making many sounds: I heard the <u>baby's cries</u>.
   - If you mean two or more babies: I heard the <u>babies' cries</u>.

8. I borrowed my bosses car for an hour because mine was in the shop.

   Bosses is plural, not possessive. Nouns need apostrophes to show ownership. I borrowed my <u>boss's</u> car for an hour because mine was in the shop.

9. I grew up in the south.

   Major regions of the United States are capitalized. I grew up in the <u>South</u>.

10. The City where Batman lives is Gotham City.

    The word *city* is capitalized only when it's part of a specific town's name. The <u>city</u> where Batman lives is Gotham <u>City</u>.

11. There are two James's and three Mindies in my class this year.

    James's implies that one guy named James owns something. We are talking about two guys, both named James. There are two <u>Jameses</u> in my class. I would guess that the three girls spell their names Mindy, not Mindie, in which case there are three <u>Mindys</u> in my class. Even though Mindy ends with a *y*, with proper nouns (people's names), we do not change the *y* to an *i* and add *es*. We leave the name as it is and just add an *s*.

Set # 2, page 18

1. Jillian remembered to bring Lydia's jacket to school but forgot her gloves.

   Whose gloves—Jillian's or Lydia's? The antecedent is unclear. Try this: Jillian remembered to bring Lydia's jacket to school but forgot to bring her own gloves.

2. They don't allow kids to throw jello at each other in the cafeteria.

   In this case, it's pretty clear who *they* are—any adult nearby! As a rule, don't use the vague *they*. Let your reader know whom you're talking about. <u>The teachers</u> don't allow kids to throw jello at each other in the cafeteria.

3. When doing a plié, the ballerina should keep her knees over her toes. You shouldn't allow your knees to turn inward or you could damage your knees and ankles.

   This paragraph switches from talking about the ballerina to using that overused *you*. The writer doesn't really mean *you the reader*; she is still talking about the ballerina. This is correct: When doing a plié, the ballerina should keep <u>her</u> knees over <u>her</u> toes. <u>She</u> shouldn't allow <u>her</u> knees to turn inward or <u>she</u> could damage <u>her</u> knees and ankles.

4. I gave Charlie a new bike and a video game; it made him happy.

   The antecedent is unclear. What is *it*? The bike? the video game? my kindness? Try this: I gave Charlie a new bike and a video game; the birthday gifts made him happy.

5. Hello. You want to speak to Esperanza? This is her.

   Would you say "her is this"? No. This is <u>she</u>.

6. We had a great time at Myrtle Beach; they have so much to do there.

   There's that sneaky *they*. Who are *they*? We had a great time at Myrtle Beach; there is so much to do there.

7. The teacher told we kids to be quiet.

   Would you say "the teacher told we to be quiet"? No. The teacher told <u>us</u> kids to be quiet.

8. We're going out to dinner alone—just Gabriela and me.

   Turn it around: Gabriela and me are going out to dinner. That's no good. It should be this: We're going out to dinner alone—just Gabriela and <u>I</u>.

9. It was him who ate all the nachos.

   Turn it around: would you say "him was it"? No. It was <u>he</u> who ate all the nachos.

10. Mom gave both of us, Elizabeth and I, money for the movie.

    Leave out some words and see how it sounds: Mom gave I money for the movie. That won't fly. It should be this: Mom gave both of us, Elizabeth and <u>me</u>, money for the movie.

11. Yuriko is a friend of Miranda's and me.

    Would you say "Yuriko is a friend of me"? No. Yuriko is a friend of Miranda's and <u>mine</u>.

12. Don't tell anyone! Keep this a secret between you and I.

    We very often hear the phrases "between you and I" and "between she and I," but they are always wrong. Turn it around. You would not say "this is between I and you." Another way to think about it is that the word *between* is a preposition. If pronouns follow a preposition (if they are the objects of the preposition) they must be in the objective case. "You" is both nominative case and subjective case; "I" is only nominative case. This is correct: Keep this a secret between you and me.

Set # 3, page 33

1. Mom fusses a lot about me trashing my room.

   Remember gerunds? *Trashing* is one of them and it takes a possessive noun or pronoun. Mom fusses a lot about <u>my</u> trashing my room.

2. When I was a kid, I swang every day on an old tire my dad hanged in a tree for me.

   There are two irregular verbs in this sentence. This is correct: When I was a kid, I <u>swung</u> every day on an old tire my dad <u>hung</u> in a tree for me.

3. I wish I'd waken up earlier.

   You have two choices: waked or woken—but not waken.

4. Bill breaks the dish when he tossed it to Laura who is standing at the sink.

   Too many different verb tenses. *Breaks* is present tense, *tossed* is past tense, *is standing* is present progressive tense, and after reading this sentence, your reader is very tense! Try this: Bill <u>broke</u> [past tense] the dish when he <u>tossed</u> [past tense] it to Laura who <u>was</u> <u>standing</u> [past progressive tense] at the sink.

5. If I was you, I'd buy that gorgeous dress.

   The word *if* is a clue that a sentence might fit the subjunctive mood, and this one does. I am not you, so this is a "what if" type of sentence. If I <u>were</u> you, I'd buy that gorgeous dress.

6. I've laid awake all night worrying about my math test.

   As you laid, did you produce any eggs? You could scramble them for breakfast or . . . oh, I bet you meant to say this: I've <u>lain</u> awake all night worrying about my math test.

7. I worked for three hours, and finally the assignment was completed.

   Keep scratching your head. Can you see the goof? This sentence switches from active voice (*I worked*) to passive voice *(the assignment was completed)*. It's not technically wrong, but in this case it's weak. This is better: I worked for three hours, and finally I completed the assignment.

8. I'm sure I lay my assignment on the teacher's desk yesterday. Where could it possibly have gone?

   Remember that *lay* works like *say* and *pay*. If it was yesterday, you said and you paid. And if it was yesterday, you laid. I'm sure I <u>laid</u> my assignment on the teacher's desk yesterday.

9. If you want to really, truly, without a doubt thrill your teacher, don't split infinitives.

   There is a very badly split infinitive (*to thrill*) in this sentence. Here's a possible solution: If you really want <u>to thrill</u> your teacher, don't split infinitives.

10. The headline read "Local Kid Won Scholarship from Pizza Hut."

    This is okay, but headlines usually use the present tense for emphasis. "Local Kid <u>Wins</u> Scholarship from Pizza Hut."

11. Brinley is dressed up today like she was Princess of Everywhere.

    Brinley is actually not Princess of Everywhere. This is a good spot for the subjunctive mood. Brinley is dressed up today like she <u>were</u> Princess of Everywhere.

12. The scientist insisted that dinosaurs were extinct.

    If we want to keep verb tenses consistent, which is usually a very good idea, this sentence is correct because both *insisted* and *were* are past tense. However, the sentence doesn't quite make sense. Some things are always true, and we use the present tense for those things. Dinosaurs <u>are</u> extinct. To say that they <u>were</u> extinct sounds as if there is a good chance they will be back next week. This is correct: The scientist insisted [past tense] that dinosaurs are [present tense] extinct.

13. Davis throwing a spit wad at Joe made Joe mad.

    Throwing is a gerund in this sentence. We almost always use the possessive case before a gerund. The way this sentence is written, the emphasis is strongly on Davis, but I would imagine Joe would have been mad at anybody throwing a spit wad at him. This is much better: Davis's throwing a spit wad at Joe made Joe mad.

Set # 4, page 41

1. The dog smells badly.

   This might be correct—it depends on what you mean.

   - If the dog stinks: The dog smells [linking verb] <u>bad</u> [adjective].
   - If the dog has a poor sense of smell: The dog smells [action verb] <u>badly</u> [adverb].

2. Of the three boys, Will runs faster.

   When there are three or more involved, use the superlative form. Of the three boys, Will runs <u>fastest</u>.

3. You sure can eat a lot of ice cream at one sitting!

   How can you eat? An adverb is needed, but *sure* is an adjective. You <u>surely</u> can eat a lot of ice cream at one sitting!

4. This is a real pretty dress.

   How pretty is the dress? An adverb is needed, but *real* is an adjective. This is a <u>really</u> pretty dress.

5. Apples turn badly if you let them sit out too long.

   Could you say that apples *seem* bad? Yes, so *turn* is a linking verb here, and it needs an adjective. Apples turn <u>bad</u> if you let them sit out too long.

6. This bottle of milk is emptier than that one.

   This is not a problem in conversation (your listener knows what you mean) or in informal writing, but it is a problem in formal writing. This is one of those all-or-nothing adjectives. Either the bottle is empty or it isn't. Both of these are correct:

   • This bottle of milk is more nearly empty than that one.

   • This bottle has less milk in it than that one.

7. I only ate three slices of pizza.

   I'm glad you only ate them. It would be a little weird if you shot baskets with them or wore those slices of pizza around your head to keep your ears warm. Oh, wait a minute, I bet you mean this: I ate <u>only</u> three slices of pizza.

8. What a nice gesture on your part to greet them so nice when they arrived.

   What kind of gesture? An adjective is needed: a nice gesture. How did you greet them? An adverb is needed: so nicely. This is correct: What a <u>nice</u> gesture on your part to greet them so <u>nicely</u> when they arrived.

9. Josh's mom hugged him real sweet and said, "Enough grammar exercises. Let's take a break."

   We can't take a break quite yet. Two adjectives sneaked into this sentence when two adverbs are needed. How did she hug him? Sweetly. How sweetly? Really sweetly. Josh's mom hugged him <u>really</u> <u>sweetly</u> and said, "Enough grammar exercises. Let's take a break."

Set # 5, page 51

1. I want new rollerblades. And I want a new game for the computer for my birthday.

   Begin a sentence with a conjunction (*and* is a conjunction) only when you want a lot of emphasis. This is not a good place to do it. I want new rollerblades and a new game for the computer for my birthday.

2. Jamie ate a plate of spaghetti, and a salad.

   When a list contains three or more items, we use a comma before the word *and*. This would be correct: Jamie ate a plate of spaghetti, two rolls, and a salad. With the example sentence, only two items are listed, so we don't use the comma. This is correct: Jamie ate a plate of spaghetti and a salad.

3. Hannah got dressed and headed out for her horseback lesson and got there early and she groomed her horse slowly.

   There are too many *and*'s in this sentence. Try this: Hannah got dressed, headed out for her horseback lesson, got there early, and groomed her horse slowly.

4. Neither Eli or Brian was able to go with us to the game.

   Neither needs *nor*. Neither Eli nor Brian was able to go with us to the game.

5. Oh, thank you, Dad! This is exactly the birthday present I was hoping for!

   The second sentence ends with a preposition. Let's see if we can change that without ruining the sentence: Oh, thank you, Dad! This is exactly the birthday present for which I was hoping! That sounds mighty stuffy to me, and the sentence as written sounds fine, so I would leave this one alone. If your teacher requires you never to end a sentence with a preposition, you could write something like this: I had been hoping for this very birthday present!

6. We drove in our new car in a hard rain through an open field over an old bridge to the house in the country where my grandmother lives.

This sentence has too many prepositional phrases in a row. There are many ways to improve it. Here's one: On a very rainy day, we drove our new car through an open field and over an old bridge until we arrived at my grandmother's country house.

7. Whoa, slow down, Princess, you're galloping too fast!

    Whoa is an interjection. It is also a very strong feeling, so it is okay for it to stand alone. This would be better: Whoa! Slow down, Princess, you're galloping too fast!

Chapter 2

Building and Punctuating Sentences

Sentences, Fragments, Phrases, and Clauses

Words are like building blocks—we can put them together in all sorts of different ways in order to make many different kinds of sentences. When we write, it is important to make complete sentences. It is a common goof to write incomplete sentences, which are also called sentence fragments.

How can you tell a complete sentence from an incomplete sentence? Usually your ear will tell you when a sentence is complete.

INCOMPLETE SENTENCE (FRAGMENT):

Two miles.
(What? Who does what for two miles? I don't get it. This is not complete.)

INCOMPLETE SENTENCE (FRAGMENT):

Two miles every day.
(I still don't get it. Two miles every day where? Why? Who? Tell me more.)

INCOMPLETE SENTENCE (FRAGMENT):

Two miles every day, rain or shine.
(I don't care about the weather! Tell me who is doing what.)

COMPLETE SENTENCE:

I run.
(This is a very simple sentence, but it has a subject [I] and a verb [run]. We know what is happening and who is doing it.)

I run two miles.
(Here is the same sentence with a little more information. There's no confusion here.)

I run two miles every day, rain or shine.
(Here is the same sentence with even more information, and it's still very clear.)

A complete sentence must have a subject and a verb.

What is a verb? (For more about verbs, see page 19.) It is a word that expresses one of two things:

- action: leap, scream, fly, swim
- state of being: appear, seem, feel, be

What is a subject? It can be any of the following things. (In each example, the subject is underlined.)

- The person who does the action in the sentence:
  <u>Will</u> serves the tennis ball.
- The thing that does the action in the sentence:
  The <u>ball</u> zips through the air.
- The person being described in the sentence:
  <u>Will</u> is happy about his powerful serve.
- The thing being described in the sentence:
  The <u>ball</u> is happy when the point is over and it can rest!

Subjects can come in many different packages. (In each example, the subject is underlined.)

- One noun as the subject: The <u>dog</u> barks.
- Two nouns as the subject (this is called a compound subject, which just means it has more than one part): The <u>dog and cat</u> are both making noise and keeping us awake.
- One pronoun as the subject: <u>She</u> can't sleep because of all the noise.

- Two pronouns as the subject (this is another type of compound subject): <u>He and she</u> are both still awake because of those noisy animals.
- A phrase: <u>Staying awake all night</u> is no fun.
- A clause: <u>What makes me mad</u> is all this noise!

Sometimes the subject "hides" from you. It's there, but you have to use your imagination.

- Run! (What do you think the subject is? It is *you*. The sentence could read *You run!* But that's not how we speak or write. We leave out the word *you*, but everybody knows it's there—hiding.)
- Eat your spinach. (When your mom or dad says this to you, you know exactly what the subject is. Who is supposed to eat the spinach? You are, and the word *you* is the hidden subject of the sentence.)

What is the difference between a clause and a phrase?

A clause has a subject and a verb; a phrase doesn't.

CLAUSE:

until I turn sixteen
(This has a subject [I] and a verb [turn], but you're left dangling, aren't you? It's not a complete sentence. This is called a dependent clause. It depends on something else to make a complete sentence.)

COMPLETE SENTENCE:

I can't drive until I turn sixteen.
(Now we know what's going on!)

PHRASE:

my big fat mouth
(We just saw that a clause has a subject and a verb. There's no verb here; this is called a phrase. It could be the start of a great sentence, but it needs some help. It needs some action.)

COMPLETE SENTENCE:

My big fat mouth got me into a bunch of trouble again.
(Now there's some action! It might not be the kind of action you like, but it makes a very clear, complete sentence.)

Let's see how complete sentences are built.

DEPENDENT CLAUSE:

when I come home from school
(This has a subject [I] and a verb [come], but your ear tells you it is not a complete sentence. What happens when you come home from school?)

PHRASE:

my brand new kitten
(There's no verb here—no action word. What does the kitten do?)

INDEPENDENT CLAUSE:

My brand new kitten jumps all over me.
(This clause is called an independent clause because it can stand as a whole, complete sentence. It doesn't depend on anything else in order to be a sentence, but we can add more if we wish.)

COMPLETE SENTENCE #1:

When I come home from school, my brand new kitten jumps all over me.

PHRASE:

my pet parrot
(There's no verb here. We need some action.)

DEPENDENT CLAUSE:

whom I call Lady Bird
(We have a subject [I] and a verb [call], but this clause doesn't make a bit of sense without more information. It's dependent on the rest of the sentence to make sense.)

PHRASE:

flies off her perch, lands on my shoulder, and begs for sunflower seeds
(Now we're cooking, but we're still confused. There's a lot of action [*flies*, *lands*, and *begs* are all verbs], but there's no subject—no noun or pronoun. We don't know who or what is doing all this.)

COMPLETE SENTENCE #2:

My pet parrot, whom I call Lady Bird, flies off her perch, lands on my shoulder, and begs for sunflower seeds.

TWO COMPLETE SENTENCES JOINED:

When I come home from school, my brand new kitten jumps all over me, and my pet parrot, whom I call Lady Bird, flies off her perch, lands on my shoulder, and begs for sunflower seeds.

(Two independent clauses are often put together. Why do we join them? To make more interesting sentences!)

Is it a sentence or is it a fragment? Sometimes it all depends on a comma.

FRAGMENT:

Soon after Lela fell asleep.
(This is a clause with a subject and a verb, but it's not a complete sentence.)

SENTENCE:

Soon after, Lela fell asleep.
(This is an introductory phrase [*soon after*] followed by an independent clause.)

There are three times when it is okay to use fragments.

- Fragments are sometimes used effectively for emphasis.

Molly thought she heard a brontosaurus outside her bedroom door. She gathered her courage and slowly walked to her door. She opened it. <u>Yes</u>! In fact, things were worse than she feared. <u>Two of them</u>!

- Fragments are fine if you're writing informal dialogue because fragments are, in fact, a common part of our everyday speech.

Syman asked, "<u>More fries for you</u>? I have some I don't want."
"<u>Sure</u>." Marshall's hand reached for the fries.
"<u>Full</u>?" asked Syman a few minutes later.
Marshall pushed away the remaining food. "<u>Yep</u>. Let's go."

- Fragments are fine with some exclamations and interjections.

<u>Oh no</u>! My pet boa constrictor just crawled into bed with Grandma!
<u>Absolutely not</u>! You may not spray paint your sister's hair purple, and don't ask me again.

What types of sentences can we build?

A **simple sentence** gives one piece of information that makes sense all by itself. The sentence can be very short or a bit longer, but it still is just one independent clause without a dependent clause or another independent clause.

The dog is howling. The cat is crying. (These are two simple sentences, two short and sweet independent clauses.)

I managed to change the lightbulb all by myself.
I broke the lamp.

A **compound sentence** is two simple sentences joined by a coordinating conjunction. Reminder: the coordinating conjunctions are the FANBOYS seven—*for, and, nor, but, or, yet, so.*

The dog is howling and the cat is crying.
I managed to change the lightbulb all by myself, but I broke the lamp.

A **complex sentence** includes one or more dependent clauses.

Although I managed to change the lightbulb all by myself, I broke the lamp. ("Although I managed to change the lightbulb all by myself" is a dependent clause. It depends on the rest of the sentence to make sense. "I broke the lamp" is an independent clause; it makes sense all by itself.)

Compound/complex sentences are a combination of compound and complex sentences.

Although I managed to change the lightbulb all by myself, I broke the lamp, and I blame the howling dog and the crying cat for the whole mess!

Why do we care about these different types of sentences with high-falutin names? One reason and one reason only: interesting writing. Write a whole paper with simple sentences. See how that looks. It is pretty boring. Every sentence is just one idea. There is no joining. There is no comparing. There is no variation. There is very little oomph. Your reader is getting very sleepy. But then, just for fun, try using diversity in sentence styles. If you have the urge, start a sentence with a conjunction; then for even more fun, throw in an unexpected surprise—perhaps a sentence fragment. If you're brave. Do you see how varying your sentence lengths and styles gives you freedom in your writing? Freedom to shine.

Road Signs: Punctuation

Some students rebel against punctuation as though putting commas and periods in the right spots is nothing more than following silly old rules that make no difference to anybody. They feel that all those rules limit their creative freedom and don't matter anyway.

Does good punctuation matter? Absolutely yes! If you want to tell a clear, interesting story, good punctuation is your best tool. Let me show you what I mean through an example. Which of these two versions do you think is clearer? Which do you enjoy reading more?

THIS ONE:

i downloaded this way cool app from—oh i can't remember; somewhere on some page of the apple app store maybe; probably; but if you googel apps and games (or something like that)) you'll probably find it and its called something like Mojo rider or maybe its /// let me think /// oh, I remember, its called Moto rider, you'll really like it i think, let me know.

OR THIS ONE:

I downloaded a really cool app that I think you're going to love. I can't remember for sure, but I probably found it on the Apple app store site, but you could google and find it easily. It's called Moto Rider. Let me know what you think!

Here is another example. Which version is clearer? Which one is easier to read and more enjoyable to read?

THIS ONE:

The last time, I was at the beach, I saw a gaw-jus—and, ooooooh do I mean gaw-jus!!—sunset. The shimmmmmmering colors of: aquamarines . . . peach . . . and . . . hmmmmm . . . oh, I guess I'd call it lavender . . . danced together on the <u>White Caps</u>—beautifully. Watching *Nature's* "artistry" made my ♥ :) quietly—yep, it did.

OR THIS ONE:

The last time I was at the beach I saw a gorgeous sunset. The shimmering colors of aquamarine, peach, and lavender danced together on the white caps in a beautiful way. Watching nature's artistry made my heart smile quietly.

Can you feel when reading the previous example what it's like to stumble as a reader? You might wrinkle your brow for a second wondering what on earth gaw-jus means, or why all the . . . ellipses? In the improved version, notice that you don't notice the punctuation or the grammar or the spelling. That's the secret of good grammar: *it disappears*! The mechanics of the sentence hide behind the scenes so that your story can shine. And your reader never stumbles.

Let's see how to use punctuation in a way that lets your stories sparkle and your creativity soar.

Periods

There are three marks of punctuation that end a sentence. The one most often used is the period. It says "STOP HERE." Back in the very old days people didn't use periods that must have been awfully confusing everything running together not knowing where one idea stops and another starts yikes makes for very difficult reading I'm glad we have periods now.

Periods are also used for a few things other than ending sentences, as we'll soon see.

The other two marks of punctuation we use to end a complete sentence are the question mark and the exclamation mark (also called the exclamation point). You can think of them as periods with special missions.

Use a period at the end of a complete sentence.
This rule is mighty easy.
I hope they are all this easy.

Use a period (decimal point) with money and percentages.
$12.56   24.6%

Use periods in URL addresses.
My main email account is on aol.com, but I use earthlink.net, too.

Use periods in some abbreviations.

When to use periods with abbreviations can be confusing. This is an area of punctuation that is changing quickly. The trend is to use fewer and fewer periods, but not all experts agree. For example, some rule books say always write U.S.A.; others say USA is fine. I'll give you some general guidelines, but when in doubt, check a good dictionary.

- These do use periods:

Months and days: Jan., Feb., Oct., Mon., Wed., Fri.

Titles: Mr., Mrs., Ms., Gen., Dr., Sen. (If you read something that was written in England, these periods are usually not used, but they are always used in the United States.)

Addresses: Ave., St., Rd., Blvd.

Initials in people's names: John Q. Public

Titles after people's names: Ph.D., M.D., Jr., Sr.

States when they are written with lowercase letters: N. Mex. (but not NM), Col. (but not CO), Cal. (but not CA)

Measurements and time (US-style): lb., oz., hr., min., mo., yr., ft., in., yd. Note that metric measurements do not take periods: g (gram), kg (kilogram), m (meter)

Some Latin abbreviations: etc. (et cetera, meaning "and so on"), i.e. (meaning "in other words"), e.g. (meaning "for example")

Time of day: Take your pick! AM, A.M., am, a.m., or AM in small caps are all okay. The most commonly used is a.m. (or p.m.), and you can't go wrong using that style.

- Acronyms are formed by taking the first letter of several words to create a new word. For example, ASAP comes from "as soon as possible" and CD/ROM comes from "compact disc read-only memory." Acronyms almost never use periods.

Agencies, companies, and organizations: NATO, FBI, NFL, IBM

Computer terms: RAM, DVD, PC

Tests: PSAT, IQ

Radio and television stations: WQDR, KABC, ESPN

Medical terms: PMS, AIDS

Directions: NE, SW, NNE

- Abbreviations and acronyms used in technology and science almost never take periods, whether they are lowercase or all caps: mph (miles per hour), mpg (miles per gallon), ppm (parts per million), STP (standard temperature and pressure), UV (ultraviolet), O (oxygen), Hg (mercury), dpi (dots per inch), UFO (unidentified flying object), DST (daylight savings time), rpm (revolutions per minute)

Do you add a period, a question mark, or an exclamation mark if the sentence ends with an abbreviation that takes periods? Periods—no. Question marks and exclamation marks—yes.

WRONG:

Danielle woke up at 7 a.m..

RIGHT:

Danielle woke up at 7 a.m.

WRONG:

Your snoring woke me up at 2 a.m!

RIGHT:

Your snoring woke me up at 2 a.m.!

Question marks
Use a question mark at the end of a sentence that asks a question.

This rule is not so hard, is it?

In a polite request (when no answer is required), the question mark is often omitted even though the sentence is phrased like a question. Use it or don't use it—it is your choice.

RIGHT:

Would you please bring us a chocolate shake and two straws?

ALSO RIGHT:

Would you please bring us a chocolate shake and two straws.

Indirect questions don't take question marks.

DIRECT QUESTION:

Is today Monday?
(This is a straightforward question.)

INDIRECT QUESTION:

I asked whether today is Monday.
(This is a statement about a question.)

WRONG:

Mei Ling asked whether the game was likely to be rained out?

RIGHT:

Mei Ling asked whether the game was likely to be rained out.

WRONG:

I wonder whether the abominable snowman is real?

RIGHT:

I wonder whether the abominable snowman is real.

ALSO RIGHT:

Is the abominable snowman real? I wonder.

If you have a question mark in the middle of a sentence, don't capitalize the word after the question mark.

What in the World is a Homophone? is a very popular children's book. (The question mark is part of the book's title.)

Will school be canceled? was on all the kids' minds.

Use a question mark to indicate uncertainty or doubt.

The author of this book lived from 1810 (?) to 1895.
(This means you're not sure that the date 1810 is correct; perhaps no one knows for sure when this particular author was born.)

Exclamation points

Use an exclamation point at the end of high-energy sentences. Here are some examples of exclamations:

DELIGHT:

Wow! This is the easiest rule in the whole book!

URGENCY:

Please help me! Watch out!

ANGER:

Drop dead! Shut up!

SURPRISE:

I can't believe it's you! This is amazing!

DISTRESS:

Oh no! This can't be happening!

EXCITEMENT:

I made straight A's on my report card!

INTENSITY:

I love you! I mean I *really* love you!

LOUD NOISES:

Bang! Crash! Boom!

STRONG COMMANDS:

Halt! Don't go one step farther!

Notice how an exclamation point changes the tone of a sentence:

LOW ENERGY:

Mom said, "No, not now."

HIGH ENERGY:

Mom said, "No! Not now!"

LOW ENERGY:

Wake up.

HIGH ENERGY:

Wake up!

Is it a question or an exclamation? Sometimes a sentence can go either way.

RIGHT:

How could you do that?

ALSO RIGHT:

How could you do that!

Beware of over-excited sentences

Some people use exclamation points all the time! Every single sentence is so excited it jumps for joy! Nothing looks sillier than a paragraph like this! Even worse than lots of exclamation points are—oh no, not those!!—double exclamation points!! In formal writing, never (and I do mean *never*!!) use double exclamation points! In fact, don't use many exclamation points at all. Not every sentence you write is exciting enough to deserve an exclamation point.

(See page 111 for using exclamation points with quotations. See page 92 for using exclamation points with parentheses.)

BRAIN TICKLERS   Set # 6

Find the goofs in these sentences and correct them.

1. Dr Austin Stevens and Gov Hartley Hsu were at the meeting.

2. I wonder if Netflix has the Bruce Lee movie I want to see?

3. Why did you bring your math teacher a bouquet of flowers instead of bringing her your overdue homework assignment, I wondered?

4. The huge dinosaurs, creatures of the distant past, pictured on the pages of history books roaming vast plains a million years ago, with their gazing eyes and huge bodies, lumbering along with no concern for what lay in their paths, creating terror wherever they roamed.

5. I want to play in the N.F.L. when I grow up.

6. Oh no, my homework is flying out the bus window.

7. Wow! I got accepted for the special summer program in Mexico!! I can't wait to go! I'm sure it will be wonderful! It's something I've wanted to do for a long time!!

(Answers are on pages 119–120.)

Semicolons

Semicolons and colons are probably the most misunderstood marks of punctuation, and very many grownups don't know how to use them correctly. That seems a little odd to me because they really aren't difficult. Semicolons and colons show us where to pause in a sentence, just like periods and commas do, but they have different jobs than periods and commas.

The main job of a semicolon is to allow two closely related sentences to work together as one sentence; they get to be cozy in the same sentence, softly divided by a semicolon rather than strongly divided by a period.

Use a semicolon between two complete sentences that are very closely related.

RIGHT:

My family is Jewish. We celebrate Chanukah but not Christmas.

BETTER:

My family is Jewish; we celebrate Chanukah but not Christmas.
(Being Jewish and celebrating Chanukah are very closely related, and that relationship is emphasized by putting them in the same sentence.)

WRONG:

My family is Jewish; not Christian.
(*Not Christian* is not a complete sentence. Use a semicolon only between two complete sentences.)

RIGHT:

My family is Jewish, not Christian.

RIGHT:

My dad is a coach at the university. We get free tickets to any sports event we want to see.
(These two sentences are very closely related.)

BETTER:

My dad is a coach at the university; we get free tickets to any sports event we want to see.

WRONG:

My dad is a coach at the university; we have some cousins who live in Texas.
(Being a coach and having cousins in Texas are not closely related.)

RIGHT:

My dad is a coach at the university. We have some cousins who live in Texas.

WRONG:

I have three dogs; and two of them are golden retrievers.
(When you use a semicolon, don't use a conjunction.)

RIGHT:

I have three dogs; two of them are golden retrievers.

ALSO RIGHT:

I have three dogs, and two of them are golden retrievers.

Use a semicolon before *however* and similar words (these words are called conjunctive adverbs) that show a relationship between two complete sentences.

WRONG:

I bet you thought you wouldn't have to learn another semicolon rule, however, you were wrong.

RIGHT:

I bet you thought you wouldn't have to learn another semicolon rule; however, you were wrong.

ALSO RIGHT:

I bet you thought you wouldn't have to learn another semicolon rule. However, you were wrong.

RIGHT:

I thought Christmas would never come; finally, it did.

RIGHT:

I ate one burger; meanwhile, the dog snuck away with the other one and devoured it.

Conjunctive adverbs are adverbs working as conjunctions, joining two sentences and showing how they relate to each other. The word *however* is one of the most commonly used ones. Here are some others: *besides, indeed, otherwise, therefore, in fact, meanwhile, in addition, consequently, nevertheless, next, still, finally, earlier, naturally, certainly, furthermore, unfortunately.* (See page 82 for info about using commas with conjunctive adverbs.)

Use a semicolon before clauses that are introduced by *for example, that is,* or *namely.*

WRONG:

Jake wants to spend the summer at camp, that is, he wants to swim, learn archery, canoe, and play lots of basketball.

RIGHT:

Jake wants to spend the summer at camp; that is, he wants to swim, learn archery, canoe, and play lots of basketball.

WRONG:

Olivia and Mallory are excellent students, for example, they both made A's on that really tough math test.

RIGHT:

Olivia and Mallory are excellent students; for example, they both made A's on that really tough math test.

PAINLESS TIP

A semicolon is stronger than a comma but slightly weaker than a period.

Use semicolons between clauses or phrases that contain a lot of commas.

CONFUSING:

Richard likes books about baseball, biplanes, and bagels, Thomas likes books about antique cars, blimps, and rare fish, and Ruth likes books about racehorses, dolls, and military jets.

BETTER:

Richard likes books about baseball, biplanes, and bagels; Thomas likes books about antique cars, blimps, and rare fish; and Ruth likes books about racehorses, dolls, and military jets.

VERY CONFUSING (IS THIS 7 PEOPLE OR 4 PEOPLE?):

We saw Meg, the captain of the basketball team, Cal, the captain of the tennis team, Ryan, the captain of the crew team, and Archer, the captain of the volleyball team.

BETTER:

We saw Meg, the captain of the basketball team; Cal, the captain of the tennis team; Ryan, the captain of the crew team; and Archer, the captain of the volleyball team.

ALSO GOOD:

We saw Meg (the captain of the basketball team), Cal (the captain of the tennis team), Ryan (the captain of the crew team), and Archer (the captain of the volleyball team).

A MESS WITHOUT SEMICOLONS:

I have relatives in Rome, Georgia, Tightsqueeze, Virginia, Athens, Ohio, and New York City.

MUCH BETTER:

I have relatives in Rome, Georgia; Tightsqueeze, Virginia; Athens, Ohio; and New York City.

Colons
Use a colon when you want to say "here comes an example" or "here's what I'm talking about."

RIGHT:

This sentence is grammatically correct: I wonder if wolves actually wolf down their pizzas the way I wolf down mine.

RIGHT:

When my older brother got to go to Disney World and I did not, I was reminded of something my mother often says: Every dog has its day.

RIGHT:

There's only one sport for me: alligator wrestling.

Notice how colons are used after the words *right* and *wrong* throughout this book. The colon says "here comes an example."

Use a colon before some lists.

A colon is needed when you use these phrases: *these are, the following, as follows,* or *these things.*

WRONG:

My favorite sports are: baseball, basketball, soccer, and football.
(Don't use a colon if the list comes right after a verb.)

RIGHT:

My favorite sports are baseball, basketball, soccer, and football.

ALSO RIGHT:

My favorite sports are the following: baseball, basketball, soccer, football, squash, racketball, tennis, lacrosse, golf, and every other game that's played with a ball.

WRONG:

I want to travel to: New York, San Francisco, Atlanta, and Montreal.
(Don't use a colon if the list comes right after a preposition.)

RIGHT:

I want to travel to New York, San Francisco, Atlanta, and Montreal.

ALSO RIGHT:

I want to travel to the following cities: New York, San Francisco, Atlanta, and Montreal.

Use a colon before subtitles of books, articles, chapters, etc.

The title of the book is *Michael Jordan: Basketball Superman.*

Use colons with expressions of time.

It's 12:15 p.m.
Philip's record for the mile is 4:06:27.

Use a colon in the greeting part of a formal letter or business letter.

To Whom It May Concern:
Dear Senator Kirkpatrick:

Use a colon in literary references between volume and page or between chapter and verse.

John 3:16 [the book of John, chapter 3, verse 16]
Encyclopedia Brittanica IV:425 [volume 4, page 425]

Use a colon with ratios.

The ratio of oil to water is 3:1. [three to one]

Use colons to indicate dialogue when you're writing a play or a script (and notice there are no quotation marks when you write dialogue this way).

Evan: I want to play baseball.
Joaquin: Great idea.
Evan: I'll get my gear and you get yours.
Joaquin: Meet you at the field.

Use a colon before a long, formal quotation.

Governor Smith stated to the press: "I think that children should study grammar for at least six hours a day. Learning to speak and write correctly is far more important than anything else—including eating. In fact, I believe that eating is a complete waste of valuable time. That is why I'm suggesting that lunch period be canceled and that students study grammar instead of eating while they are at school."

Fortunately, Governor Smith then said, "April Fools!"

Use a colon after words such as *caution, wanted,* or *note.*

Caution: slippery floor
Wanted: part-time waitresses and waiters
Note: We're almost finished with colons!

Capitalize the first word after a colon if it begins a complete sentence—and if you want to. Either way is okay; it's your choice.

WRONG:

These are the ingredients: Apples, olives, sugar, onions, artichokes, and chocolate. Sounds yummy, doesn't it?
(*Apples* does not begin a complete sentence.)

RIGHT:

These are the ingredients: apples, olives, sugar, onions, artichokes, and chocolate. Sounds yummy, doesn't it?

RIGHT:

I'm sure you know the old saying about apples: An apple a day keeps the doctor away.
(*An* begins a complete sentence.)

ALSO RIGHT:

I'm sure you know the old saying about apples: an apple a day keeps the doctor away.

BRAIN TICKLERS   Set # 7

Find the goofs in these sentences and correct them.

1. I want to see the new ninja movie, I want to see the new Spider-Man movie, too.

2. When you go to the store, please pick up: apples, bread, and juice.

3. Mom said that only one thing will earn me an increase in allowance: A consistently clean room.

4. I love the words brouhaha, googaloo, and flabbergasted, the names Vanessa, Charlotte, and Cassandra, the states Iowa, Idaho, and Illinois, but not the foods anchovies, olives, and eggplant.

5. I like chocolate cake; my dad cooks great spaghetti.

6. This is the weather forecast for tomorrow, heavy rain, gusty winds, and a chance of flooding.

7. Evan kept talking in class, in addition, he kept blowing and popping huge bubbles with his bubble gum.

(Answers are on pages 120–121.)

Commas

Commas have many jobs to do in the English language, and they are used more than any other mark of punctuation. Before we look at how to use them, let's look at just how important they are. Does it really matter whether your commas are in the right places? You bet it does! Check these out:

SAY WHAT?

The dog said my dad is scratching at the door and needs to go out for a walk.

THAT'S MORE LIKE IT:

The dog, said my dad, is scratching at the door and needs to go out for a walk.

SAY WHAT?

The girls, who sold the most Girl Scout cookies, won a trip to the beach. (This implies that there was another group also selling cookies—maybe boys or parents.)

THAT'S MORE LIKE IT:

The girls who sold the most Girl Scout cookies won a trip to the beach.

UH-OH:

Let's eat Grandma.

WHEW:

Let's eat, Grandma.

Use a comma between two complete sentences that are joined by a coordinating conjunction.

Here are the seven coordinating conjunctions: *and, but, for, or, so, nor, yet.*

RIGHT:

My sister's name is Lily. My brother's name is Lucas.
(These are two complete, correct sentences.)

BETTER:

My sister's name is Lily, and my brother's name is Lucas.

RIGHT:

I rushed home. I finished my homework before soccer practice.

BETTER:

I rushed home, and I finished my homework before soccer practice.

WRONG:

I am very good in Spanish, and in French.
(*And in French* is not a complete sentence.)

RIGHT:

I am very good in Spanish and in French.

ALSO RIGHT:

I am very good in Spanish, and I'm good in French.
(*I'm good in French* is a complete sentence.)

When the two independent clauses are very short, you have a choice—comma or no comma:

RIGHT:

Allene slept late, but James got up early.

ALSO RIGHT:

Allene slept late but James got up early.

⚡ CAUTION—Major Mistake Territory!

A comma all by itself is not strong enough to separate two independent clauses. Be alert! This is a very common comma goof.

WRONG:

We went to the beach last summer, I learned to surf.

RIGHT:

We went to the beach last summer. I learned to surf.

ALSO RIGHT:

We went to the beach last summer; I learned to surf.

ALSO RIGHT:

We went to the beach last summer, and I learned to surf.

(For when *not* to use commas with conjunctions, see page 45.)

Use a comma after conjunctive adverbs (these are adverbs working as conjunctions—they link two complete sentences and show how the two are related).

Here are some conjunctive adverbs: *however, finally, furthermore, indeed, meanwhile, nevertheless, therefore, unfortunately.*

I thought I made a C+ on the test; however, I made a B+.
I didn't study very much; nevertheless, I made a good grade.
I might not be so lucky next time; therefore, I'm going to study right now!

(What are semicolons doing in these sentences? See page 75.)

Use a comma after most introductory phrases and clauses.

Because my mother forgot to pack me a dessert, I ate your cookie.
Being a sugar freak, I have to have at least one cookie a day.

How do you tell what's introductory and what's not? Find the main subject and verb of the sentence. Whatever comes before the subject and verb is usually an introduction.

Because my mother forgot to pack me a dessert, I [subject] ate [verb] your cookie.

We frequently begin sentences with dependent clauses such as "because my mother forgot to pack me a dessert." They are introductions to the sentence and are followed by a comma.

Don't fall for the temptation to use a comma just because the subject and verb are far apart.

WRONG:

Eating too many cookies or other sweet things, can give you the sugar jitters.

RIGHT:

Eating [subject] too many cookies or other sweet things can give [verb] you the sugar jitters.

When the introduction is short, you can omit the comma if you choose.

RIGHT:

In June I will be going to camp.

ALSO RIGHT:
In June, I will be going to camp.

But beware. What can happen if you don't use commas after introductory phrases and clauses—even short ones? Confusion, that's what!

CONFUSING:
After eating my cat hiccups.
(Do you eat cats often?)

CLEAR:
After eating, my cat hiccups.

Notice that if you reverse the order of this sentence (putting the subject and verb first), you no longer have an introduction and no longer need a comma.

My cat hiccups after eating.

Use commas to emphasize an adverb.

RIGHT:
Laney ran fast and got home before her mother.

MORE EMPHASIS:
Laney ran, fast, and got home before her mother.

RIGHT:
He fell off his bicycle hard after he skidded on loose gravel.

MORE EMPHASIS:
He fell off his bicycle, hard, after he skidded on loose gravel.

Use commas when adjectives come after the noun.

My tennis racket, freshly strung and shiny new, will surely bring me good luck in the tournament.
My language arts teacher, kind of heart and generous of spirit, will surely give me an A if I learn all these comma rules.

Use commas in lists.

RIGHT:
We studied math, history, health, and grammar.

OKAY:

When I go on vacation, I like playing tennis and rollerblading and trying to beat my dad at putt-putt.

MUCH BETTER:

When I go on vacation, I like playing tennis, rollerblading, and trying to beat my dad at putt-putt.

Is it okay to omit the last comma? Most newspapers omit it (in order to save space), but many good writers use it.

OKAY:

This train goes to Norfolk, Washington, New York, and Boston.

ALSO OKAY:

This train goes to Norfolk, Washington, New York and Boston.

Take your pick, but be consistent and be aware of potential confusion when you don't use that last comma.

SAY WHAT?

I like peanut butter and jelly, macaroni and cheese and bananas covered with chocolate.
(Macaroni and cheese and bananas covered with chocolate? Yuck!)

MUCH BETTER:

I like peanut butter and jelly, macaroni and cheese, and bananas covered with chocolate.

Use commas with cities and states. Notice both commas.

I was born in Atlanta, Georgia, on Valentine's Day.

Use commas with addresses. Notice there is no comma between the state and the zip code.

She lives at 225 Valley Road, Hope, Maine 04847.

Use commas in numbers over 999.

There were 24,567 deliriously happy fans at the football game.

EXCEPTIONS:

years (2016), addresses (4627 Main St.), and telephone numbers

Use commas with direct quotations (what someone says).

"There's a big bug in my bed," yelled Sofia.
"I'm eight years old," Kwan said, "and I'm in third grade."

Use commas only with direct quotations, not with indirect quotations.

DIRECT QUOTATION:

Kate said, "I want to gallop off into the sunset."
(This is a straightforward quotation of what Kate said, using her exact words.)

INDIRECT QUOTATION:

Kate said that she wants to gallop off into the sunset.
(This is my report of what Kate said, but not necessarily using her exact words. Notice there is no comma after *Kate said*.)

WRONG:

Parker said, that she wants to swim with dolphins someday.

RIGHT:

Parker said that she wants to swim with dolphins someday.

(See pages 108–112 for more about punctuating quotations.)

Use commas when speaking directly to someone (this is called direct address).

Keith, it's time to brush your teeth.
I've told you twice, boys and girls, to do your homework.

Use commas with dates.

RIGHT:

I was born on Thursday, December 27, 1996, in Boston.
(This is the most commonly used style. Notice all three commas. It's a very common mistake to leave out one or two.)

ALSO RIGHT:

I was born in December 1996 in Boston.
(When you use just the month and year, no comma is needed.)

ALSO RIGHT:

I was born on 27 December 1996 in Boston.
(Notice with this style, no commas are used.)

Use a comma before and/or after an interjection.

(See page 51 for more about interjections.)

Wow, what a beautiful dress.
Hey, that's my lunch! No, I don't want to share my lunch with you.
Well, well, well. My goodness, you've grown so much.

Use a comma when the last part of the sentence is a question.

You were late, right?
You are going, aren't you?

Use commas sometimes between consecutive adjectives (two or more in a row) describing the same noun.

RIGHT:

It was a dark, cold, dreary night.
(*Dark*, *cold*, and *dreary* all describe the noun *night*.)

ALSO RIGHT:

It was a cold September night.
(*Cold* and *September* both describe the noun *night*, but no comma is used.
When do you use a comma and when don't you? Use a comma wherever
the word *and* would sound right.)

RIGHT:

I bought some expensive, stylish white tennis shoes.

- Does this sound okay: expensive *and* stylish shoes? Yes, so the comma is
  needed between them.
- Does this sound okay: stylish *and* white shoes? That one's iffy. I would
  leave out the comma.
- Does this sound okay: white *and* tennis shoes? No, so don't use a comma
  there.

Here's another trick: use a comma when you could switch
the order of the adjectives and the sentence would still sound right.

RIGHT:

I bought white tennis shoes.
(Does this sound okay: I bought tennis white shoes? No, so no comma is
needed.)

RIGHT:

It was a dark, cold, dreary night.
(Does this sound okay: It was a cold, dark night? Yes, so the comma is
needed. Does this sound okay: It was a dreary, cold night? Yes, so that
comma is also needed.)

Alert! Don't put a comma before the noun.

WRONG:

I ate a beautiful, ripe, delicious, red, firm, apple.

RIGHT:

I ate a beautiful, ripe, delicious, red, firm apple.

Use commas before and after some Latin abbreviations.

I like stone fruits, e.g., peaches and nectarines, more than I like berries.
(*E.g.* means "for example.")

A vet works with many types of animals—dogs, cats, horses, cows, etc.
(*Etc.* means "and so forth.")

Use commas before and after parenthetical expressions.

By-the-way phrases are words inserted into a sentence giving information or thoughts that are not absolutely essential.

I reminded Mom, in case she'd forgotten, that I really want a digital camera for my birthday.
They usually cost, if you get a good deal, about $200.
Since she's the best mom in the world, or at least that's what I tell her to get her to do whatever I want, I'm sure she'll get me one.

(See page 95 for more about parenthetical expressions.)

Use commas after greetings and before closings in friendly letters.

GREETING:

Dear Kareem,

GREETING:

Dear Mom,

CLOSING:

Love,

CLOSING:

Sincerely,

WRONG:

Dear Governor Sutton,

RIGHT:

Dear Governor Sutton:
(This is not a friendly letter. It's a formal letter, and a colon should be used.)

Use a comma to show that two parts of a sentence are being contrasted.

I ordered pizza, not lasagna.

Use commas between repeated words.

That airplane ride was bumpy, bumpy, bumpy.

Use commas to indicate omitted words.

I ordered chicken; Amanda, fish.
(This means "I ordered chicken; Amanda ordered fish.")

Tonight I will study math; tomorrow, Spanish.
(This means "Tonight I will study math; tomorrow I will study Spanish.")

Use commas with titles when they come after (but not before) the person's name.

Notice the commas before and after the title.

RIGHT:

Jacques Roche, DVM, is a famous cockroach veterinarian.

BUT NO COMMAS HERE:

Dr. Roche is a famous cockroach veterinarian.

Use commas before and after appositives (an appositive explains who or what the noun is).

RIGHT:

Our principal, John Bossman, gave a great speech.
(The subject is *principal*. The appositive, *John Bossman*, tells more about who the subject is.)

BUT NO COMMAS HERE:

Principal John Bossman gave a great speech.
(In this case *John Bossman* is part of the subject. If you leave out his name, the sentence doesn't make sense.)

RIGHT:

Katie Stevens, the best ballerina in the performance, shone as the star of the evening.
(*The best ballerina in the performance* explains who Katie Stevens is.)

BUT NO COMMAS HERE:

Ballerina Katie Stevens shone as the star of the evening.

(*Ballerina Katie Stevens* is all one unit, not one phrase telling more about another phrase.)

RIGHT:

Joshua Zinn, world-famous aardvark trainer, will be in town next week to demonstrate his great skills.
(*World-famous aardvark trainer* explains who Joshua Zinn is.)

BUT NO COMMAS HERE:

World-famous aardvark trainer Joshua Zinn will be in town next week to demonstrate his great skills.
(*World-famous aardvark trainer Joshua Zinn* is all one unit, not one phrase telling more about another phrase.)

Pulling it all together

Here's the bad news: there are a lot of comma rules to remember. Now the good news: if you remember one little "secret," you will use commas correctly almost all the time. That secret is that in many cases commas occur where you would pause for a little breath if you were saying the sentence out loud. When we speak with other people (little breath), we often pause in order to get our meaning across (little breath), and we don't run all our words together. Check this out:

NO BREATH:

No way I'm going to eat those beets.

BREATH:

No, I don't really want another serving of beets, although they were mighty good.

Say these sentences out loud and you will hear or even "feel" places where you need a little pause to help the sentence make sense.

NO BREATH:

Oh no! My ice cream just slid off the cone and onto the floor.

BREATH:

Oh, no, I don't want chocolate ice cream today. I want strawberry.

NO BREATH:

My new laptop has a flash drive with more storage than I'll probably ever be able to use.

BREATH:

My new laptop, which my best-mom-in-the-world mom got me for Christmas, has a flash drive with more storage than I'll probably ever be able to use.

Remember to listen for that little pause, that tiny breath, and commas will become much easier to use.

BRAIN TICKLERS   Set # 8

Find the goofs in these sentences and correct them.

1. At the fair, I ate cotton candy, a caramel apple and, a foot-long hot dog.

2. I pigged out on food at the fair, and got a stomachache as a result.

3. Dad was tired but, he kept driving until we finally arrived at the beach.

4. Mom said, "I'm warning you! I can't take much more of this honey."

5. I was just about to spray paint the coffee table and the cat jumped on it.

6. We will meet on Monday December 26, 2021.

7. People from Raleigh, North Carolina often vacation at Myrtle Beach, South Carolina.

8. I admit that yes I did put that turtle in the toilet.

9. The tall guy on the basketball team Legs Long is my neighbor.

10. My husband Jim is here.

11. Everyone, who hasn't finished the test, must stay after school to finish it.

12. I know I said I'd be there at 9:00, but hey I didn't count on twelve inches of snow.

13. I called you Lindsey just to say hello.

14. Whitney bought a lacy, very, sequined, dark, blue dress.

(Answers are on pages 122–124.)

Parentheses
Use parentheses to set off parenthetical expressions from the main part of the sentence.

What is a parenthetical expression? It is by-the-way information (inserted in the middle of a sentence, like this) that isn't absolutely necessary. Notice in all the following examples that you could leave out the parenthetical information and the sentence would still make sense, but if you want to include it, you can "tuck it in" inside parentheses. Here are some examples of parenthetical expressions:

- An explanation: The academic year (this year that's August 20–June 13) includes 180 school days.
- A translation: I paid 489 Mexican pesos (about $25) for dinner.
- A clarification: I was surprised when your cat pocket dialed (or paw dialed) my cell phone.
- A feeling: School is canceled (yippee!) today.
- A joke or play on words: We're having chocolate mousse (no, not chocolate moose) for dessert.
- An opinion: We're all out (and I hope we remain out) of livermush.
- A list: Some of my favorite foods (candied asparagus, fried pears, and pickled chicken) were on the menu.

Don't use parentheses to ramble.

LOUSY WRITING:

Yesterday (Thursday) I went to baseball practice (boy, was my throwing arm sore from Wednesday's practice!), got there a few minutes late (hey, just a few minutes), and got fussed at by the coach (gimme a break) who said this was my second time late this week (but once was my mom's fault) and I'd better shape up (okay, okay, I'll try).

Punctuating sentences with parentheses can sometimes be tricky.

Notice the correct position of the comma or the period in these sentences.

WRONG:

When I'm hungry (like now,) all I can think about is food.

WRONG:

When I'm hungry, (like now) all I can think about is food.

RIGHT:

When I'm hungry (like now), all I can think about is food.

WRONG:

I took my girlfriend out to dinner (if you can call splitting a hot dog dinner.)

RIGHT:

I took my girlfriend out to dinner (if you can call splitting a hot dog dinner).

WRONG:

Don't pay attention to Sam. (He doesn't know what he's talking about). Pay attention to me.

RIGHT:

Don't pay attention to Sam. (He doesn't know what he's talking about.) Pay attention to me.
(If a complete sentence is inside the parentheses, put the period inside.)

RIGHT:

Don't pay attention to Sam (he doesn't know what he's talking about); pay attention to me.
(Even though the parenthetical comment is a complete sentence, I've chosen to embed it in a larger sentence. Notice the correct punctuation—no capital letter to begin it and no period.)

Here are a few more examples of punctuating with parentheses.

Notice carefully where periods, commas, question marks, and exclamation points belong.

I'm angry (really angry!) about your going to the movie without me.
(Only the parenthetical comment is an exclamation.)

We loved the movie (it's great!).
(Only the parenthetical comment is an exclamation. In this example, notice the order: exclamation point, parenthesis, period.)

What an exciting movie (*Cliffhanger*)!
(In this case, the whole sentence is an exclamation.)

I'm sad (that doesn't surprise you, does it?) about your going to the movie without me.
(Only the parenthetical comment is a question.)

Did you enjoy the movie (it was a Narnia movie, wasn't it?) enough to go see it again?
(Both the parenthetical comment and the whole sentence are questions.)

I'm sad about your going to the movie without me. (Promise you won't do it again?)

(The parenthetical comment is a whole sentence and is not embedded in a larger sentence. Punctuate it as you would any other sentence.)

I'm sad about your going to the movie without me (promise you won't do it again?) because I really wanted to see it.
(The parenthetical comment is a whole sentence, but this time it is embedded in a larger sentence. Don't use a capital letter to begin it unless the first word is a word that must always be capitalized; for example, someone's name.)

I'm sad about your going to the movie without me (please don't do it again) because I really wanted to see it.

Notice that when you embed a whole sentence in another sentence, if it's a question, you use the question mark. If it's an exclamation, you use the exclamation point. If it's a statement, do not use the period.

I'm happy (are you?) that there's no school today.
I'm happy (ecstatic is more like it!) that tomorrow is my birthday.
I'm happy (you are probably miserable) that an itsy bitsy spider is swimming in your soup.

Brackets
Use brackets to insert explanations or instructions that are not actually part of the sentence.

The correct way to write the sentence is this: Each [singular subject] of the boys is [singular verb] here.
Batman said, "My sidekick [Robin] is on his way."

Dashes

Dashes add emphasis—a bit of dash, you might say—and often make sentences stronger or spunkier than conjunctions, commas, or semicolons do. Dashes say "hold on, wait a second—something interesting is coming."

Some writers think dashes indicate sloppy writing—no way! Dashes are energetic marks of punctuation—they can show excitement or surprise—they're spunky and lively. However, if you use too many of them—as I've done here—your writing looks like it's covered with snail tracks—not to mention chopped up and silly. Pick your spots for dashes carefully—don't overdo it.

Use a dash to link two parts of a sentence.

OKAY:

Always buckle your seat belt because it's the law.

ALSO OKAY:

Always buckle your seat belt; it's the law.

STRONGER:

Always buckle your seat belt—it's the law.

OKAY:

I gave you my last $20, so don't waste it.

ALSO OKAY:

I gave you my last $20; don't waste it.

STRONGER:

I gave you my last $20—don't waste it.

Use a pair of dashes to emphasize by-the-way, parenthetical expressions.

My grandmother bought me a puppy—an adorable little bulldog!—for my birthday.
I've lived in Portland—the one in Oregon, not Maine—all my life.

Use a dash to set off a long appositive (a description of who or what the subject is).

RIGHT:

I love *coq au vin*, a French version of chicken stew that is full of delicious herbs and veggies.

BETTER:

I love *coq au vin*—a French version of chicken stew that is full of delicious herbs and veggies.

Use dashes to set off an appositive that is full of commas.

CLEAR:

My dog, Butch, is hungry.

CONFUSING:

My dogs, Butch, Molle, and Teddy, are hungry.

BETTER:

My dogs—Butch, Molle, and Teddy—are hungry.

LESS EMPHASIS BUT ALSO GOOD:

My dogs (Butch, Molle, and Teddy) are hungry.

Use dashes to set off abrupt breaks that you want to emphasize.

I got an A—holy cow—on the exam!

I wore my fur coat—fake fur, of course—to the dance.

Use a dash in dialogue to show hesitation or a break in the flow of the sentence.

Davis said, "I definitely studied enough for the test—or I think I studied enough—I probably studied nearly enough—well, I hope I studied enough."

Use a dash to sum up a list or an idea.

Red, white, and blue—those are the American colors.

Victory—that's the name of the game.

PAINLESS TIP

Some writers make dashes with no space before or after—like this. Others prefer to leave one space before and after dashes — like this. If you are typing on a computer that won't make a dash, use two hyphens -- like this.

Parenthetical (by-the-way) expressions
Should you use parentheses, commas, or dashes?

Think of parentheses as hiding information (de-emphasizing it) while dashes highlight information—emphasizing it. Think of commas as being matter-of-fact, neither highlighting nor hiding information. In each example, the parenthetical information can be left out, but it adds interest and zest to the sentence. Notice the subtle differences in these sentences. In each case, I prefer the third example, but all of these sentences are correct. Which do you prefer?

The tennis team (especially Martha) played great.

The tennis team, especially Martha, played great.

The tennis team—especially Martha—played great.

The tennis team, except for Pete, played great.
The tennis team—except for Pete—played great.
The tennis team (except for Pete) played great.

Isabela looked beautiful, incredibly beautiful, in her prom gown.
Isabela looked beautiful (incredibly beautiful) in her prom gown.
Isabela looked beautiful—incredibly beautiful—in her prom gown.

If you eat too much ice cream (as I've done today), you'll get sick.
If you eat too much ice cream—as I've done today—you'll get sick.
If you eat too much ice cream, as I've done today, you'll get sick.

BRAIN TICKLERS   Set # 9

Find the goofs in these sentences and correct them.

1. My math teacher—Dr. Arith Metic—absolutely loves to watch students squirm when he writes painfully long equations on the blackboard.

2. Ryan (he's my neighbor) and Whitney (that's his wife) are going to go scuba diving (not just snorkeling but scuba diving with all the gear) in Florida (they wanted to go to some Caribbean island but it was too expensive) on some cool coral reefs where they hope to see lots of exotic fish (I hope no sharks!).

3. There is only one thing I need to be happy (or I should say really happy:) chocolate.

4. I am excited (really excited!) about the party.

5. I want three things for Christmas, some computer games, rollerblades, and ice skates.

6. Never text while you're driving; it's extremely dangerous.

7. What, give up whining?

8. When you come to my house (You can still come, can't you)? remember to bring your iPad.

(Answers are on pages 124–126.)

Hyphens

A hyphen is a tiny mark of punctuation that works like sticky tape: it joins two things together for the sake of making our meaning clear. For example, it would be confusing to write that my cat was born on 4 16 2020, but my meaning is very clear when I write that my cat was born on 4-16-2020. The 4 and the 16 and the 2020 are meant to go together, and the hyphens join them quite nicely. Similarly, notice how confusing this headline is: "Rescue Squad Helps Dog Bite Victim." And notice how a tiny hyphen can make sense out of nonsense: "Rescue Squad Helps Dog-Bite Victim." The words *dog* and *bite* are meant to be joined, almost as though they are one word but not quite, and the hyphen performs that job well.

Use a hyphen with some prefixes, especially *all-*, *co-*, *ex-*, *great-*, numbers, and capital letters.

all-knowing, all-around
co-conspirator, co-author
ex-husband, ex-convict
great-grandmother, great-uncle
35-cent piece of candy, 40-foot tree
T-shirt, PG-rated

Use a hyphen when a word would be confusing or hard to read without it.

CONFUSING:

shelllike (three l's in a row)

CLEAR:

shell-like

CONFUSING:

Anne recovered from the flu and recovered her living room chair.

CLEAR:

Anne recovered from the flu and re-covered her living room chair.

CONFUSING:

The fried chicken salesman was hot, greasy, and unhappy.

CLEAR:

The fried-chicken salesman was hot, greasy, and unhappy.

Use a hyphen with double last names or titles.

Mary Scott-Simons is secretary-treasurer of the club.

Use hyphens (or slashes) with dates.

RIGHT:

11-5-20

ALSO RIGHT:
11/5/20

Use a hyphen with compound numbers from 21 to 99.

twenty-two
thirty-five

Use hyphens in compound adjectives if they come before the noun they describe.

(A compound adjective is two or more words that belong together and are read as if they were one word.)

the 15-year-old girl
up-to-date technology
eighth-grade students
a drive-me-completely-nuts class

If the compound adjective comes after the noun, don't use hyphens.

The girl is 15 years old.
The technology is up to date.
The students are eighth graders.
This class is going to drive me completely nuts.

Be careful—some words that may look like compound adjectives are not.

WRONG:
Muffy is a healthy-happy kitten.
(These are two separate, independent adjectives. Either could be used alone and the sentence would make sense.)

RIGHT:
Muffy is a healthy, happy kitten.

WRONG:
Baseball is a frequently-played sport.
(*Frequently* is an adverb describing *played*, not part of a compound adjective.)

RIGHT:
Baseball is a frequently played sport.

Sometimes a little hyphen can make a huge difference.

CONFUSING:

We sold the little used bicycle for $30.

DO YOU MEAN:

We sold the little, used bicycle for $30.

OR DO YOU MEAN:

We sold the little-used bicycle for $30.

Use hyphens to spell out words.

She said, "My name is Kacey, K-a-c-e-y."

Use hyphens to show faltering speech.

Oh no! Y-y-you t-t-took my ph-ph-phone!

Use hyphens in some compound words (two or more separate words that we think of as one unit).

This is tricky territory and the rules are always changing. *Today* used to be spelled *to-day*, and *baseball* used to be *base-ball.*

Is it cheerleader, cheer leader, or cheer-leader?
Is it president-elect, president elect, or presidentelect?
Is it spring break, springbreak, or spring-break?
Is it self-awareness, self awareness, or selfawareness?
Is it baby talk, babytalk, or baby-talk?
(In all five examples, the first spelling is correct.)

Is it *vice-president* or *vice president?* Both are correct. Sometimes you can be right either way—sometimes not even all dictionaries agree whether to use a hyphen. Choose a good dictionary and trust it. And be consistent; if you use the spelling *vice-president* in one place, use the same spelling throughout your paper.

Use hyphens for hyphenating words.

Hyphenation is important when you're writing in narrow columns (for example, a newspaper article) and need to divide words. Most of the time when you're writing by hand or on a computer, there's no need to hyphenate. When you do hy-phen-ate, you must break the word prop-er-ly. If you are un-sure where a word breaks, look it up in your dic-tion-ary.

REMINDER

This is a hyphen-
This is a dash—
This is okay as a dash--

Apostrophes
Use an apostrophe with nouns to indicate ownership.

(See page 6 for more on making nouns possessive.)

Alonso's baseball   my sister's cat
the Harrises' car   the women's dresses

But don't use an apostrophe with possessive pronouns (pronouns that show ownership).

WRONG:

Who's bat is this?

RIGHT:

Whose bat is this?

CAUTION—Major Mistake Territory!

Write it right and earn big points with your teacher. Don't confuse these:

there's—theirs
you're—your
who's—whose
it's—its

WRONG:

When your writing a paper, its very important to use these words correctly. Whose going to take you're writing seriously if theirs a goof in every sentence?

RIGHT:

When you're writing a paper, it's very important to use these words correctly. Who's going to take your writing seriously if there's a goof in every sentence?

For more information about *its* and *it's*, see page 161.

Use an apostrophe to indicate missing letters or numbers.

10 of the clock = 10 o'clock   I like them = I like 'em
1993 = '93   it is = it's
we were not = we weren't   you are = you're

Almost never use an apostrophe in plural words.

Using an apostrophe to create a plural word is one of the most frequent mistakes you'll see, and you'll see that goof everywhere: huge billboards, signs, menus, advertisements, posters. I love looking for them.

Baked chicken with pea's and mashed potato's
Parking for Taxi's and Bus's Only
Open on Sunday's
No dog's allowed!

The taxis and buses don't own anything, and the dogs don't own anything. Those words are plurals, not possessives, and the apostrophes look very silly.

WRONG:

Both boy's and girl's are invited to try out for the swim team.

RIGHT:

Both boys and girls are invited to try out for the swim team.

WRONG:

tomato's for sale

RIGHT:

tomatoes for sale

WRONG:

The Brown's live here.

RIGHT:

The Browns live here.

WRONG:

I grew up in the 1990's.
(Never use an apostrophe with years, unless you're abbreviating them, as above.)

RIGHT:

I grew up in the 1990s.

Almost never use an apostrophe with plural abbreviations and acronyms.

The recipe calls for 1 lb. of ground beef and 2 lbs. of ground pork.
Walmart is having a huge sale on TVs, DVDs, and UFOs!

EXCEPTION: When abbreviations contain capital letters and periods, such as M.D.'s and Ph.D.'s, an apostrophe is used.

Do use an apostrophe with these plurals.

NUMBERS OTHER THAN YEARS:

There are three 9's on this page.
There are three 9s on this page.
(With numbers other than years, either way is correct.)

WORDS USED AS WORDS:

There are too many *but*'s in that sentence.

ALPHABET:

Mississippi is spelled with four *s*'s, four *i*'s, and two *p*'s.

Ellipses

Use an ellipsis to indicate that some words have been left out of a quotation.

The governor said, "It is very important for our children . . . that the school year be extended . . . and that they go to school . . . 360 days a year."

Uh-oh, sounds bad. But you have to be wary with ellipses. What if the newspaper reporter left out some crucial words? What if what the governor really said was this:

"It is very important for our children to have plenty of play time. Some people argue that the school year be extended, but I feel that our kids work hard enough and that they go to school enough days. Nobody should go to school 360 days a year!"

Use an ellipsis to indicate that something unwritten came earlier.

" . . . I do," said Mimi.

Use an ellipsis to indicate a sentence trailing off.

Imagine this as the final sentence of a book chapter—it entices you to turn the page to read what happens next:

Tom and Carlos were camping in the woods, asleep in their tent, when they heard it—the sound . . .

Use an ellipsis to indicate a long, slow break.

LONG, SLOW BREAK:

There it was again . . . that soft but eerie sound.

FAST, CRISP BREAK:

There it was again—that loud, crashing sound.

Underlining and italics

Use italics or underlining for names of ships, aircraft, and spacecraft; also for names of albums, books, magazines, newspapers, movies, television shows, operas, plays, and other large works.

The New York Times	The New York Times
Star Wars	Star Wars
Lord of the Rings	Lord of the Rings

Use quotation marks for the names of songs, poems, and other small works. See page 107 for more.

Use italics or underlining for emphasis.

I really mean it this time: *Don't bite the dog!*
Guess what *I* got for Christmas—a laptop!

Use italics or underlining for foreign words.

RIGHT:

It's your birthday! I wish you *feliz cumpleaños*!

ALSO RIGHT:

It's your birthday! I wish you feliz cumpleaños!

Some words are so common in English that they aren't considered foreign anymore; for example, patio, kindergarten, quiche, and salsa. But what about piñata and sombrero? Are they foreign or not? It's your call—or consult your dictionary.

> ☝ **PAINLESS TIP**
>
> Italics are usually preferable to underlining, and most computers can make italics. Use underlining only when you're writing by hand, using a mobile app that can't make italics, or want underlining for a special purpose.

Use italics or quotation marks for words used as words.

RIGHT:

Pneumonia is a tough word to spell.

ALSO RIGHT:

"Pneumonia" is a tough word to spell.

Asterisks and bullets

***These are asterisks.
• • • These are bullets.

Asterisks are used to say "look at the bottom of the page for an additional note."* Asterisks have traditionally been used to highlight or separate information, particularly items in a list. Bullets, however, are now being used more often than asterisks for this purpose. (See page 91 for an example of a bulleted list.)

Slashes
Use slashes or hyphens with dates.

RIGHT:

1/1/06

ALSO RIGHT:

1-1-06

Use a slash with certain pairs of words as a sort of shorthand to mean *and* or *or*.

he/she = he or she
the soup/salad lunch = the soup and salad lunch

---

* You get the idea? If you see an asterisk, look at the bottom of the page to find out what the extra information is.

Use a slash with fractions.

$2\frac{1}{2}$ $^{16}\!/_{17}$

Use a slash to mean *per*.

60 miles/hour = 60 miles per hour
36 candles/box = 36 candles per box
2 aspirin/day = 2 aspirin per day

BRAIN TICKLERS   Set # 10

Find the goofs in these sentences and correct them.

1. I saw two elephant's waltzing in my front yard.

2. The waiter confessed, "You're dinner is ready and there's is ready, but I've forgotten who's dinner is who's. What did you order?"

3. Bill called his sisters names.

4. Cary is great at do-it yourself projects.

5. Kristopher wanted a new jacket . . . he couldn't find one he liked . . . . so . . . he found someone who could teach him how to make it himself.

6. This computer is to-die-for!

7. We ate three quarter pound lobsters.

8. There was a long line at the restaurant drive through, so I sat in my car with the air-conditioning running and read a news paper.

9. My dad reads "The Wall Street Journal" every day.

10. I liked your article <u>Techniques for Rollerblading on Gravel, Ice, and Snow</u>.

11. I ordered beef. My French friend ordered the same, but he called it boeuf.

12. Debbie bought a 10 foot Christmas tree this year.

13. Could I please see the kids menu?

14. "I a'int ready, so ya'll go on without me," said Fred.

(Answers are on pages 126–128.)

Quotation marks

Use quotation marks to enclose what someone says.

When you use someone's exact words, that is called a direct quotation.

Mario said, "Get me a Coke," and Elena replied, "Get it yourself."
My math teacher said, with a frown on her face, "Three plus three does not equal 33, and I suspect you were pulling my leg."

Do not use quotation marks with indirect quotations.

(See page 85 for more about indirect quotations.)

WRONG:

Becca said that she "wants a dwarf killer whale for a pet."
(I'm telling you about what Becca said, but I'm not using her exact words.)

RIGHT:

Becca said that she wants a dwarf killer whale for a pet.

ALSO RIGHT:

Becca said, "I want a dwarf killer whale for a pet."
(Now I'm using Becca's exact words; this is a direct quotation.)

WRONG:

I told Ming to, "Finish his homework."

RIGHT:

I told Ming to finish his homework.

If a quotation is half direct and half indirect, don't use quotation marks unless you are using the person's exact words and you want to emphasize the quotation.

WRONG:

Ella Kate referred to her horse as, "A magnificent white steed."

RIGHT:

Ella Kate referred to her horse as a magnificent white steed.

ALSO RIGHT:

Ella Kate referred to her horse as a "magnificent white steed."
(Notice there is no comma and *magnificent* is not capitalized.)

ALSO RIGHT [DIRECT QUOTE]:

Ella Kate said, "My horse is a magnificent white steed."

Thoughts or questions in someone's mind (in other words, ideas not spoken out loud) do not need quotation marks.

WRONG:

"Will I survive this bungee jump?" Brian wondered.

RIGHT:

Will I survive this bungee jump? Brian wondered.

WRONG:

I've asked myself many times "why eat vegetables?"

RIGHT:

I've asked myself many times, why eat vegetables?

Use quotation marks to suggest doubt or sarcasm.

You call this a "bicycle"? I call it a pile of rusty metal.
The teacher said we did "okay" on the test—whatever that means.

Use quotation marks (not underlining or italics) for the names of songs, poems, magazine articles, newspaper articles, short stories, chapters of books, and other small works.

SONG:

"The Star-Spangled Banner"

ARTICLE:

"Tar Heel Women Win Soccer Nationals"

Use quotation marks for definitions.

One definition of the word *squash* is "to press or smash something flat"; another is "a sweet fruit juice"; another is "a summertime vegetable"; yet another is "a game played with rackets and a small rubber ball."

The word *scuttlebutt* means "rumor or gossip," so "What's the scuttlebutt?" means "What's the latest gossip?"

Use quotation marks for sayings.

"Don't count your chickens before they hatch" means don't act as if something you hope might happen is a sure bet.

Use quotation marks for labels, markings, signs, etc.

Notice there are no commas before or after these quotation marks.

I'm confused. This stoplight says "stop" and that one says "go."
Stamp the receipts "paid."
Label this container "good toys" and that one "broken toys."

Use quotation marks to indicate the clever or silly use of a word.

I love the "flowers" you made out of ribbon and beads.
Ted really "spazzed out" when the teacher asked him to recite the "preambulator" to the Constitution in front of the class.
I am "a-maized" how good this corn tastes!

Don't be too cute. It is a common "goofy goof" to overuse quotation marks in an attempt to be "qute" and clever, drawing attention to certain words in a "ha-ha" or sarcastic ("gimme a break") way. Some students put every single "slangy" word in quotes, and anything that's the least "itsy bitsy" silly gets the "squiggly" little marks, too. Before long their papers look really "b-a-d" when what they intended was to look really "r-a-d."

More on quotations

Punctuating quotations can be tricky, but if you follow these four simple examples, you'll get it right at least 90 percent of the time.

Sofia said, "Hello."
• Use a comma before the opening quotation mark.
• Use a capital letter to begin the quotation.
• Put the period inside the closing quotation mark.

Sofia said, "Hello," and I asked, "What's up?"
• Use a comma before the opening quotation mark.
• Use a capital letter to begin the quotation.
• Use a comma (not a period) after *hello* because the sentence is not over yet.
• Use a comma before the opening quotation mark of the second person's quotation.
• Use a capital letter to begin the second quotation because there is a new speaker.

"I'm hungry," Sofia said, "and I'm dying for some chocolate-covered pickles. Do you have any around here?"
• Put the comma after *hungry* inside the quotation mark.

- Use a comma (not a period) after *said* because Sofia's first sentence is still going on.
- Do not capitalize *and*—this is not a new sentence. This is still part of Sofia's first sentence.
- Do not put a closing quotation mark after *pickles*. Sofia is still talking. Don't use the closing quotation mark until she's finished.
- Capitalize *do*; it begins a new sentence, Sofia's second sentence.

"Help!" cried Sofia. "Without chocolate-covered pickles, I'll surely starve."

- Use a period (not a comma) after *Sofia* because Sofia is saying two separate sentences.
- Capitalize *without*; it begins a new sentence that Sofia is saying.

Commas and periods always go inside the quotation mark.

WRONG:

I said to my dog, "Sit", and amazingly he did.

RIGHT:

I said to my dog, "Sit," and amazingly he did.

WRONG:

The title of the song is "River of Dreams".

RIGHT:

The title of the song is "River of Dreams."

Colons and semicolons always go outside the quotation mark.

WRONG:

Catherine said, "I'll clean my room;" now we'll see if she means it.

RIGHT:

Catherine said, "I'll clean my room"; now we'll see if she means it.

WRONG:

Mom uttered the first rule of "parental law:" *just because I say so!*

RIGHT:

Mom uttered the first rule of "parental law": *just because I say so!*

If you have a quotation within a quotation, use single quotation marks around it.

RIGHT:

Sawyer said, "My mom said, 'No way!'"

RIGHT:

Sawyer said, "My mom said, 'No way!' so I guess we can't go."

If only yes or no is quoted, you don't have to use quotation marks.

RIGHT:

Jamal said yes.

ALSO RIGHT:

Jamal said, "Yes."

If several different speakers are quoted, start a new paragraph for each new speaker.

All the boys had gathered at Levi's house. Levi said, "Does anyone want to play basketball?"

"Sure," replied Owen. "Where's the ball?" He ran toward the basketball hoop but couldn't find a ball there.

"There's one in the garage," called Levi. "I'll get it." Levi went to get the ball while the other kids began to choose teams.

"I want to be on Owen's team!" shouted Max.

"Me, too," said Logan.

"Well, I want to be on Levi's team," chimed in Bob.

Quotations that are questions can be tricky.

Notice when the question mark goes inside the quotation mark and when it goes outside.

If only the quotation is a question:

WRONG:

Branch asked, "Is that you"?

RIGHT:

Branch asked, "Is that you?"

If the whole sentence is a question but the quotation is not:

WRONG:

Are you the person who said, "No onions for me?"

RIGHT:

Are you the person who said, "No onions for me"?

If both the quotation and the sentence are questions:

WRONG:

Are you the person who asked, "Are there vampires out tonight"?

RIGHT:

Are you the person who asked, "Are there vampires out tonight?"

Quotations that are exclamations can also be tricky.

Notice when the exclamation point goes inside the quotation mark and when it goes outside.

If only the quotation is an exclamation:

WRONG:

I think he's the one who yelled, "Help"!

RIGHT:

I think he's the one who yelled, "Help!"

If both the quotation and the sentence are exclamations:

WRONG:

Oh my gosh, someone is screaming, "Help!"!

RIGHT:

Oh my gosh, someone is screaming, "Help!"

If the whole sentence is an exclamation but the quotation is not:

WRONG:

I was furious when he smugly said, "Drop dead!"

RIGHT:

I was furious when he smugly said, "Drop dead"!

If a quotation from one person is longer than one paragraph, there is no closing quotation mark until the very end of the quotation.

Each new paragraph begins with an opening quotation mark, but there is no closing quotation mark until the speaker is completely finished.

Charlie said to his math teacher, "I did study for the exam. I really did.

"It's just that I had a slight problem. You see, my math book is printed in Japanese. I know it sounds strange, and it's the only book of its kind, but it's a fact.

"If you don't believe me, I'll be glad to show you.

"So, you see, if you had asked the questions in Japanese, I would have known the answers and probably would have made an A.

"You do believe me, don't you?"

BRAIN TICKLERS   Set # 11

Find the goofs in these sentences and correct them.

1. "Hi, Julie", said Sean.

2. Julie replied, "Hi, Sean".

3. "I'm looking for my shoes," said Sarah, "I'm sure I left them somewhere in this room."

4. "I would do almost anything for you, Mom," said Josh. "Except take out the trash."

5. What does the saying a penny saved is a penny earned mean?

6. I found a box in the attic labeled, "Baseball cards," and another labeled, "Old photos."

7. "How are you?", I asked Erica.

8. I read the poem "Ode to a Toad;" I liked it a lot.

9. Phoebe asked whether she "could sleep over at Eliza's house."

10. I was sad when she yelled, "I hate you"!

11. Did you ask, "Do you really want me to eat this slimy okra"?

12. Dad gave me "big bucks" (two "whole" dollars) to spend at the "bead store."

13. Emma said, "Madison said, yes, I'll help you, but she didn't."

14. "When will it be time for dinner?" I wonder.

(Answers are on pages 128–130.)

Highlights: Abbreviations, Symbols, Numbers, and Emphasis
@ # $ √ 18 ≤ % 6.5 ¢ ≠ +
Abbreviations and symbols
If you're writing a note to yourself or a letter to a friend, use any symbols and abbreviations you wish.

However, in formal writing avoid most symbols and abbreviations.

SAY WHAT?

On Mon. I traveled E along I-40 past RDU headed for E. NC. FYI, I was transporting 1/2 doz. newborn puppies (valued at > $100 @) to a kennel, and I wanted to get them to their dest. ASAP.

MUCH BETTER:

On Monday I traveled east along Interstate 40 past Raleigh-Durham airport headed for eastern North Carolina. For your information, I was transporting six newborn puppies (valued at over $100 each) to a kennel, and I wanted to get them to their destination as soon as possible.

WEAK:

I felt OK about my brother + sister tagging along.

BETTER:

I felt okay about my brother and sister tagging along.

WEAK:

There are 12 in. in a ft. and 36 in. in a yd.

BETTER:

There are 12 inches in a foot and 36 inches in a yard.

Do use abbreviations with most titles.

They are much easier to read than spelling out the entire title.

RIGHT BUT VERY AWKWARD:

We invited Mister Chan, Mistress Chan, Ms. Sutton, Doctor Stevens, and Bill Stevens, Junior, to our party.

RIGHT AND EASIER TO READ:

We invited Mr. Chan, Mrs. Chan, Ms. Sutton, Dr. Stevens, and Bill Stevens, Jr., to our party.
(Note: *Ms.* exists only as an abbreviation.)

How to write numbers

If you're writing a paper for science class or math class, you would obviously use many more symbols and numerals than you would if you're writing a poem or a short story for language arts class.

RIGHT FOR MATH CLASS:

$2 + 2 = 4$

RIGHT FOR LANGUAGE ARTS CLASS:

Two plus two equals four.

WRONG FOR LANGUAGE ARTS CLASS:

The 2 are $\neq$

RIGHT FOR LANGUAGE ARTS CLASS:

The two are not equal.

Different writers have different styles when it comes to numbers.

Some write out almost all numbers (even big, hard-to-read numbers such as *one thousand four hundred and twenty*). Most newspapers write out the numbers one through nine and use numerals for 10 and up. An important point to remember is this: Be consistent!

INCONSISTENT:

At the zoo we saw thirty-two zebras, 14 elephants, twenty-seven iguanas, and 13 lions.

CONSISTENT:

At the zoo we saw 32 zebras, 14 elephants, 27 iguanas, and 13 lions.

When writing numbers, make life easy for your reader.

RIGHT BUT HARD TO READ:

I'd love to have three thousand six hundred and seventy cats.

RIGHT AND EASY TO READ:

I'd love to have 3,670 cats.

If you wish, write out numbers above ten as long as they are easy to read.

EASY TO READ:

I'd love to have two cats—two hundred cats—even two thousand cats.

EASY TO READ:

Claire says she has dreamed at least a million times about being a tennis pro.

Don't start a sentence with a numeral.

WRONG:

12,477 fans attended the game.

RIGHT BUT HARD TO READ:

Twelve thousand four hundred and seventy-seven fans attended the game.

RIGHT AND EASY TO READ:

There were 12,477 fans at the game.

Here's how to avoid confusion with side-by-side numerals:

CONFUSING:

There were 16 6-foot men playing basketball.

CLEAR:

There were 16 six-foot men playing basketball.

ALSO CLEAR:

There were sixteen six-foot men playing basketball.

Numbers with time

RIGHT BUT HARD TO READ:

Jesse ran the course in three hours, eighteen minutes, and five seconds.

RIGHT AND EASY TO READ:

Jesse ran the course in 3 hours, 18 minutes, and 5 seconds.

RIGHT:

I woke up at six o'clock in the morning.

RIGHT AND EASIER TO READ:

I woke up at 6:00 a.m.

Numbers with ages

RIGHT:

I am twelve years old and my mom is thirty-seven years old.

EASIER TO READ:

I am 12 years old and my mom is 37 years old.

Numbers with money

Right but hard to read	Right and easy to read
four dollars and fifty cents	$4.50
three point six million dollars	$3.6 million
$200,000,000,000	$200 billion
$0.47	47 cents

Numbers with dates

WRONG:

Today is June 19th.
(We say the *th*, but we don't write it with dates that come after the month.

RIGHT:

Today is June 19.

ALSO RIGHT:

Today is the 19th.

Always use numbers with addresses.

WRONG:

She lives at three sixty-four Cedar Valley Court.

RIGHT:

She lives at 364 Cedar Valley Court.

Numbers with measurements, weights, and temperatures

RIGHT:

Her baby is a beautiful seven-pound, ten-ounce boy.

EASIER TO READ:

Her baby is a beautiful 7-pound, 10-ounce boy.

RIGHT:

It's only sixteen degrees outside!

EASIER TO READ:

It's only 16 degrees outside!

With ordinals (1st, 2nd, 3rd, etc.), write them out if they are only one word, but use numerals if they contain more than one word.

INFORMAL:

Wesley was the 1st person ever to water ski on his head.

BETTER:

Wesley was the first person ever to water ski on his head.

INFORMAL:

Makoto ranks 10th in his school and 20th in the state.

BETTER:

Makoto ranks tenth in his school and twentieth in the state.

RIGHT BUT HARD TO READ:

Joe is ranked thirty-second in the state, and Mia is ranked one hundred twenty-sixth.

EASIER TO READ:

Joe is ranked 32nd in the state, and Mia is ranked 126th.

> ## PAINLESS TIP
>
> Should 100 be a *hundred* or should it be *100*? It all depends. Consider the context: is this a math paper or a poem? Is it a physics final exam or a love letter? Usually go with whatever is quicker for the eye to grab and, therefore, easier for your reader to read.

CREATING EMPHASIS

How can you draw attention to certain words or phrases in your writing? Notice how "Creating Emphasis" is written—exciting, isn't it? Well, you can't use fancy fonts all the time. Here are some ways you can do it with punctuation.

Imagine that your cousin Jeff has been missing for three years. One night there's a knock at the door. You open the door and . . .

When I opened the door, I couldn't believe my eyes. It was Jeff.
I couldn't believe my eyes: it was Jeff.
I couldn't believe my eyes: it was Jeff!

I couldn't believe my eyes—it was Jeff!
I couldn't believe my eyes. *It was Jeff!*
I couldn't believe my eyes . . . Jeff!
I couldn't believe my eyes—JEFF!
I couldn't believe my eyes—<u>JEFF</u>!

Be careful not to overdo emphasis. Too little makes your writing dull, but too much makes your writing look silly.

Speaking of silly, check this out:

Holy cow! I could *hardly* believe how incredibly <u>lucky</u> I was!! I played HARD this season, but I really didn't expect to win (yes, win!!) the coveted *t-r-o-p-h-y*. What a surprise! I was in total awe . . . and I do mean *total*, as in—wow!—**mega-total**.

A bit too much emphasis, don't you think?

BRAIN TICKLERS   Set # 12

Find the goofs in these sentences and correct them.

1. We moved to Tenn. from Va.

2. 1996 is the year I was born.

3. A football field is 100 yd. long.

4. I ate sixteen pizzas, 6 orders of fries, seventy-seven potato chips, and ½ a pecan pie.

5. There are 2 2-toed sloths in the zoo.

6. We live at sixty-four Elm Street.

7. I was born on December 27th, 2002.

8. Don't use symbols & abbrev. in formal writing.

9. Wow! SUPER DOOPER g!o!!!!!y! The chapter is over!!

(Answers are on page 131.)

BRAIN TICKLERS—THE ANSWERS

Set # 6, page 73

1. Dr Austin Stevens and Gov Hartley Hsu were at the meeting.

   This would be correct if you were writing in England, but in the USA, we use periods after Dr. and Gov. Dr. Austin Stevens and Gov. Hartley Hsu were at the meeting.

2. I wonder if Netflix has the Bruce Lee movie I want to see?

   This is an indirect question; change the question mark to a period. I wonder if Netflix has the Bruce Lee movie I want to see.

3. Why did you bring your math teacher a bouquet of flowers instead of bringing her your overdue homework assignment, I wondered?

   The question mark is in the wrong place. Why did you bring your math teacher a bouquet of flowers instead of bringing her your overdue homework assignment? I wondered.

4. The huge dinosaurs, creatures of the distant past, pictured on the pages of history books roaming vast plains a million years ago, with their gazing eyes and huge bodies, lumbering along with no concern for what lay in their paths, creating terror wherever they roamed.

   That's a fine bunch of words, but it's not a sentence. A simple word change here or there would make all the difference. The huge dinosaurs, creatures of the distant past pictured on the pages of history books, roamed vast plains a million years ago; with their gazing eyes and huge bodies, they lumbered along with no concern for what lay in their paths, creating terror wherever they roamed.

5. I want to play in the N.F.L. when I grow up.

   Most abbreviations and acronyms that contain all capital letters don't need periods. This is better: I want to play in the NFL when I grow up.

6. Oh no, my homework is flying out the bus window.

   This is not wrong, but this high-energy sentence deserves an exclamation mark or two. Oh no! My homework is flying out the bus window!

7. Wow! I got accepted for the special summer program in Mexico!! I can't wait to go! I'm sure it will be wonderful! It's something I've wanted to do for a long, long time!!

   Even though this is an excited paragraph, all the exclamation marks detract from the excitement more than they enhance it. How about this: Wow! I got accepted for the special summer program in Mexico! I can't wait to go. I'm sure it will be wonderful, and it's something I've wanted to do for a long, long time.

Set # 7, page 79

1. I want to see the new ninja movie, I want to see the new Spider-Man movie, too.

   Two complete, separate sentences are joined by a comma. That won't do! A comma is not strong enough for the job. These two sentences are closely related, so a semicolon would be a good choice. Both of these are correct:
   - I want to see the new ninja movie; I want to see the new Spider-Man movie, too.
   - I want to see the new ninja movie. I want to see the new Spider-Man movie, too.

2. When you go to the store, please pick up: apples, bread, and juice.

   Don't use a colon if the list comes immediately after the verb, as it does here. (The verb is *pick up*.) Both of these are correct:
   - When you go to the store, please pick up apples, bread, and juice.
   - When you go to the store, please pick up these things: apples, bread, and juice.

3. Mom said that only one thing will earn me an increase in allowance: A consistently clean room.

   Capitalize the first word after a colon only if it begins a complete sentence. *A consistently clean room* is not a complete sentence.

Mom said that only one thing will earn me an increase in allowance: a consistently clean room.

4. I love the words brouhaha, googaloo, and flabbergasted, the names Vanessa, Charlotte, and Cassandra, the states Iowa, Idaho, and Illinois, but not the foods anchovies, olives, and eggplant.

All those commas make this sentence very confusing! This sentence needs a healthy dose of semicolons. I love the words brouhaha, googaloo, and flabbergasted; the names Vanessa, Charlotte, and Cassandra; the states Iowa, Idaho, and Illinois; but not the foods anchovies, olives, and eggplant.

5. I like chocolate cake; my dad cooks great spaghetti.

These two sentences are not closely related, so the semicolon is wrong. Here are two possible ways to clean it up:
- I like chocolate cake. My dad cooks great spaghetti.
- Two of my favorite foods are chocolate cake and my dad's great spaghetti. (Notice that I have created a link between chocolate cake and spaghetti, so it now makes sense to put them in the same sentence.)

6. This is the weather forecast for tomorrow, heavy rain, gusty winds, and a chance of flooding.

Commas are gentle pauses, not strong alerts that important information is on the way. This is the weather forecast for tomorrow: heavy rain, gusty winds, and a chance of flooding.

7. Evan kept talking in class, in addition, he kept blowing and popping huge bubbles with his bubble gum.

These are two separate sentences (two independent clauses) that are joined by "in addition." The phrase "in addition" is working as a conjunctive adverb, and it needs a semicolon. That's not always easy to recognize or remember. What is easier to remember is that a comma is never strong enough to join two separate sentences (independent clauses) unless it has a coordinating conjunction to go with it. Both of these are correct:
- Evan kept talking in class, and [coordinating conjunction] he kept blowing and popping huge bubbles with his bubble gum.
- Evan kept talking in class; in addition, he kept blowing and popping huge bubbles with his bubble gum.

Set # 8, page 90

1. At the fair, I ate cotton candy, a caramel apple and, a foot-long hot dog.

    What's the comma doing after *and?* In lists, put a comma before *and*, not after. At the fair, I ate cotton candy, a caramel apple, and a foot-long hot dog.

2. I pigged out on food at the fair, and got a stomachache as a result.

    These are not two separate sentences joined by a conjunction. (*Got a stomachache as a result* is not a sentence.) Both of these are correct:
    *   I pigged out on food at the fair and got a stomachache as a result.
    *   I pigged out on food at the fair, and I got a stomachache as a result.

3. Dad was tired but, he kept driving until we finally arrived at the beach.

    These are two separate sentences joined by a conjunction, but the comma is in the wrong place. It always goes before the conjunction, never after it. Dad was tired, but he kept driving until we finally arrived at the beach.

4. Mom said, "I'm warning you! I can't take much more of this honey."

    Uh-oh. Mom is pretty mad at those bees. Sure glad it's not me! Wait a minute . . . unless what she really means is "I can't take much more of this, honey."

5. I was just about to spray paint the coffee table and the cat jumped on it.

    Remember how commas are like little breaths? Without a tiny pause, it sounds as though the cat is about to get painted some unflattering color. I was just about to spray paint the coffee table, and the cat jumped on it.

6. We will meet on Monday December 26, 2021.

    There's a comma missing. Put one after *Monday*.

7. People from Raleigh, North Carolina often vacation at Myrtle Beach, South Carolina.

   There's a comma missing. Put one after *North Carolina*.

8. I admit that yes I did put that turtle in the toilet.

   Two commas are missing. I admit that, yes, I did put that turtle in the toilet.

9. The tall guy on the basketball team Legs Long is my neighbor.

   Legs Long is an appositive—it tells more about *the tall guy on the team*. It needs commas. The tall guy on the basketball team, Legs Long, is my neighbor.

10. My husband Jim is here.

    I would guess that many adults would not see anything wrong with this sentence. Parenthetical (by-the-way) information needs to be set off from the rest of the sentence in some way. If the information is not set off, it is considered to be crucial to the sentence. Writing that "my husband Jim is here" clearly implies that I have more than one husband and I am talking specifically about the one named Jim. Hmmm, not what I meant to say. My husband, Jim, is here = My husband (whose name, by the way, is Jim) is here.

11. Everyone, who hasn't finished the test, must stay after school to finish it.

    The commas around the clause *who hasn't finished the test* indicate that this is a by-the-way clause—in other words, you can delete it and the sentence will still make sense. Let's try it: *Everyone must stay after school to finish it.* Oops, that's not what you meant to say, is it? This is correct: Everyone who hasn't finished the test must stay after school to finish it.

12. I know I said I'd be there at 9:00, but hey I didn't count on twelve inches of snow.

    Put commas before and after interjections. I know I said I'd be there at 9:00, but, hey, I didn't count on twelve inches of snow.

13. I called you Lindsey just to say hello.

    Did you call Lindsey on the phone to say hello or did you yell out "Lindsey!" to somebody in order to say hello? When we're talking directly to someone (that's called direct address), we use commas before and after the person's name. I think this is what you mean: I called you, Lindsey, just to say hello.

14. Whitney bought a lacy, very, sequined, dark, blue dress.

    Where would you put *and*'s? "Very and sequined" is clearly not good; *very* is an adverb modifying the adjective *sequined*, so that comma should go. "Lacy and very sequined" sounds fine, so let's leave that comma in. "Dark blue" sounds good, but "dark and blue" does not, so that comma should go. This is correct: Whitney bought a lacy, very sequined, dark blue dress.

Set # 9, page 96

1. My math teacher—Dr. Arith Metic—absolutely loves to watch students squirm when he writes painfully long equations on the blackboard.

   This sentence is not wrong, but the dashes give the teacher's name a lot of emphasis. Is that really where the emphasis belongs in this sentence? I think students squirming about the long equations is the emphasis. This looks better to me: My math teacher, Dr. Arith Metic, absolutely loves to watch students squirm when he writes painfully long equations on the blackboard.

2. Ryan (he's my neighbor) and Whitney (that's his wife) are going to go scuba diving (not just snorkeling but scuba diving with all the gear) in Florida (they wanted to go to some Caribbean island but it was too expensive) on some cool coral reefs where they hope to see lots of exotic fish (I hope no sharks!).

   There are too many parentheses in this sentence. They make the sentence look chopped up with too many rambling thoughts thrown in, and they make it very hard to read. Either tie the thoughts together or throw some of them out of the sentence. This is much better: My neighbor Ryan and his wife, Whitney, are going scuba diving on some cool coral reefs in Florida. They are hoping to see some beautiful exotic fish.

3. There is only one thing I need to be happy (or I should say *really* happy:) chocolate.

    The colon is in the wrong place. There is only one thing I need to be happy (or I should say *really* happy): chocolate.

4. I am excited (really excited!) about the party.

    This is okay, but parentheses "hide" information. With this much emphasis, dashes might be better. I am excited—really excited!—about the party.

5. I want three things for Christmas, some computer games, rollerblades, and ice skates.

    The comma after *Christmas* won't do. It's much too weak for the job. Here are two ways to clean up this sentence:
    - I want three things for Christmas—some computer games, rollerblades, and ice skates.
    - I want three things for Christmas: some computer games, rollerblades, and ice skates.

6. Never text while you're driving; it's extremely dangerous.

    This is okay, but it could take even more emphasis. Dashes create more emphasis than semicolons do. Never text while you're driving—it's extremely dangerous.

7. What, give up whining?

    This is the perfect sentence (okay, it's a fragment) for a dash, and it is actually a little bit confusing without one. What—give up whining? No actor could say that line without sass. Can you hear how that dash makes your voice rise a bit and puts some punch into the words? That's the emphasis that a well-placed dash can deliver.

8. When you come to my house (You can still come, can't you)? remember to bring your iPad.

    There are two mistakes. "You can still come, can't you?" is a complete sentence, but it is not standing alone. It is tucked inside another sentence, inside parentheses. The first *you* should not be capped, and the question mark should go inside. This is correct: When you come to my house (you can still come, can't you?) remember to bring your iPad.

Set # 10, page 105

1. I saw two elephant's waltzing in my front yard.

    Elephants should be plural, not possessive. Delete the apostrophe. I saw two elephants waltzing in my front yard.

2. The waiter confessed, "You're dinner is ready and there's is ready, but I've forgotten who's dinner is who's. What did you order?"

    Yikes! What a mess. Did you catch all these apostrophe goofs? Possessive pronouns *never* take apostrophes. <u>Your</u> dinner is ready and <u>theirs</u> is ready, but I've forgotten <u>whose</u> dinner is <u>whose</u>.

3. Bill called his sisters names.

    Very tricky. The apostrophe [*sisters* or *sister's* or *sisters'*] makes all the difference. This sentence is correct if you mean that Bill called his two sisters bad names. But maybe you mean one of these:
    * Bill called [yelled out] his [one] <u>sister's</u> [Katie's] names [Katie, Katherine, Kat, little sis].
    * Bill called [yelled out] his two <u>sisters'</u> [Katie's and Becca's] names.

4. Cary is great at do-it yourself projects.

    Do-it-yourself is a compound adjective describing *projects*. It is meant to be read as one word, so it needs hyphens. It is a common mistake to stop short and hyphenate only part of a compound adjective. Cary is great at <u>do-it-yourself</u> projects.

5. Kristopher wanted a new jacket . . . he couldn't find one he liked. . . . so . . . he found someone who could teach him how to make it himself.

    Some people get into the habit of using an ellipsis for almost every type of punctuation, especially commas, semicolons, dashes, and periods. And often they use as many dots as they feel like, when three dots are all that are needed. This sentence doesn't need any ellipses at all. Kristopher wanted a new jacket; he couldn't find one he liked, so he found someone who could teach him how to make it himself.

6. This computer is to-die-for!

   If a compound adjective comes before the noun, use hyphens. (For example: This is a <u>to-die-for</u> computer!) If a compound adjective comes after the noun, don't use hyphens. This is correct: This computer is <u>to die for</u>!

7. We ate three quarter pound lobsters.

   Tricky! Do you mean you ate several lobsters that each weighed three-quarters of a pound? Or that you ate 3 quarter-pound lobsters? Both of these are correct:
   - We ate three quarter-pound lobsters.
   - We ate three-quarter-pound lobsters.

8. There was a long line at the restaurant drive through, so I sat in my car with the air-conditioning running and read a news paper.

   Some compound nouns are written as two words, some are one word, and some are hyphenated. Check your dictionary! In this case, this is right: There was a long line at the restaurant <u>drive-through</u>, so I sat in my car with the <u>air conditioning</u> running and read a <u>newspaper</u>.

9. My dad reads "The Wall Street Journal" every day.

   Names of newspapers should be underlined or, better, put in italics. Both of these are correct:
   - My dad reads *The Wall Street Journal* every day.
   - My dad reads <u>The Wall Street Journal</u> every day.

10. I liked your article <u>Techniques for Rollerblading on Gravel, Ice, and Snow</u>.

    Large works such as books are underlined or written in italics; small works are put in quotation marks. An article is considered a small work. I liked your article "Techniques for Rollerblading on Gravel, Ice, and Snow."

11. I ordered beef. My French friend ordered the same, but he called it boeuf.

    Use italics or underlining for foreign words. Both of these are correct:
    *   My French friend ordered the same, but he called it *boeuf.*
    *   My French friend ordered the same, but he called it <u>boeuf.</u>

12. Debbie bought a 10 foot Christmas tree this year.

    A hyphen is needed. Debbie bought a 10-foot Christmas tree this year.

13. Could I please see the kids menu?

    Are you sure that's what you want to see? The kids menu is a menu of dishes made from goat meat (baby goats are called kids). The kid's menu is a menu made for or by one particular kid. I bet what you really want to see is the <u>kids'</u> menu.

14. "I a'int ready, so ya'll go on without me," said Fred.

    Is *ain't* a word? Not in formal writing. However, we hear it used often in informal conversation, and you might write it frequently in dialogue. If you do use it, put the apostrophe in the right place. *Ain't* is used to mean *are not* (they ain't ready yet), *am not* (I ain't ready yet), or *is not* (she ain't ready yet either), so the apostrophe clearly indicates that the letter *o* is left out of *not*, just the same as if we were writing *don't*. Is *y'all* a word? I'm a southerner, so I say you betcha it is! Not for formal writing, perhaps, but it's a very convenient way to create a plural form of the pronoun *you* without saying *you guys*. We southerners beg all the rest of you, please put the apostrophe in the right place. *Y'all* is clearly short for *you all*, so why on Earth do so many folks spell it *ya'll?*

Set # 11, page 112

1. "Hi, Julie", said Sean.

    In the United States, we always put commas *inside* the quotation mark. "Hi, Julie," said Sean. If you are reading something that was written in England, you might see the comma sometimes placed outside the quotation mark. However, most U.S. grammar books, teachers, and editors would see that as an error.

2. Julie replied, "Hi, Sean".

   Always put periods *inside* the quotation mark. Julie replied, "Hi, Sean." Again, in England it is sometimes acceptable to put the period *outside* the quotation mark, but this style is not considered okay in the United States.

3. "I'm looking for my shoes," said Sarah, "I'm sure I left them somewhere in this room."

   These are two separate sentences spoken by Sarah. The two sentences should be separated by a period. "I'm looking for my shoes," said Sarah. "I'm sure I left them somewhere in this room."

4. "I would do almost anything for you, Mom," said Josh. "Except take out the trash."

   Josh is saying only one sentence, so *except* should not be capitalized (it doesn't begin a new sentence) and there should not be a period after *Josh* (the sentence isn't over). "I would do almost anything for you, Mom," said Josh, "except take out the trash."

5. What does the saying a penny saved is a penny earned mean?

   Use quotation marks for expressions. What does the saying "a penny saved is a penny earned" mean?

6. I found a box in the attic labeled, "Baseball cards," and another labeled, "Old photos."

   Just as periods are used for a few things other than ending sentences (*www.google.com*, for example), quotation marks are used for a few things other than quotations, and the way we punctuate around them is different from the way we punctuate quotations. These are not quotations, they are labels. With labels, titles, signs, or markings, punctuate this way: I found a box in the attic labeled "baseball cards" and another labeled "old photos."

7. "How are you?", I asked Erica.

   What's the comma doing in this sentence? The question mark takes the place of the comma. "How are you?" I asked Erica.

8. I read the poem "Ode to a Toad;" I liked it a lot.

   Semicolons go *outside* quotation marks, even though commas and periods go inside. Why the difference? It's just another one of those quirky things about the English language, or I should say the American language. In England, writers are not so rigid about this rule, but in the United States we are. This is correct: I read the poem "Ode to a Toad"; I liked it a lot.

9. Phoebe asked whether she "could sleep over at Eliza's house."

    This is an indirect quotation. I'm telling you what Phoebe said, but I'm not quoting her exact words. Therefore, quotation marks are not used. Phoebe asked whether she could sleep over at Eliza's house.

10. I was sad when she yelled, "I hate you"!

    The quotation is an exclamation, but the whole sentence is not. I was sad when she yelled, "I hate you!"

11. Did you ask, "Do you really want me to eat this slimy okra"?

    The question mark is in the wrong place. In this sentence, both the quotation and the whole sentence are questions. Using two question marks would look weird, so we use only one, and we use it with the quotation. This is correct: Did you ask, "Do you really want me to eat this slimy okra?"

12. Dad gave me "big bucks" (two "whole" dollars) to spend at the "bead store."

    "Big bucks" indicates you're joking or being sarcastic; that one is okay. The other two ("whole" and "bead store") are unnecessary and silly. This is better: Dad gave me "big bucks" (two whole dollars) to spend at the bead store.

13. Emma said, "Madison said, yes, I'll help you, but she didn't."

    This is a quotation within a quotation. We use regular (double) quotation marks for the first quotation and single quotation marks for the second one. Emma said, "Madison said, 'Yes, I'll help you,' but she didn't."

14. "When will it be time for dinner?" I wonder.

    Thoughts and questions in the mind (not spoken out loud) don't take quotation marks. When will it be time for dinner? I wonder.

Set # 12, page 118

1. We moved to Tenn. from Va.

   In formal writing, don't use many abbreviations. This is better: We moved to Tennessee from Virginia.

2. 1996 is the year I was born.

   It looks awkward to start a sentence with a number. This is correct: I was born in 1996.

3. A football field is 100 yd. long.

   Write out the word *yards*. A football field is 100 yards long.

4. I ate sixteen pizzas, 6 orders of fries, seventy-seven potato chips, and ½ a pecan pie.

   The numbers are inconsistent and hard to read. There are several styles that are okay, but this one is best: I ate 16 pizzas, six orders of fries, 77 potato chips, and half a pecan pie.

5. There are 2 2-toed sloths in the zoo.

   The two *twos* side by side is hard to read. There are two 2-toed sloths in the zoo.

6. We live at sixty-four Elm Street.

   Even though this might look very fancy and formal, never spell out numbers in addresses. We live at 64 Elm Street.

7. I was born on December 27th, 2002.

   That *th* makes the number 27 an ordinal. That's fine if you're saying "I was born on the 27th," but in this case because you're writing an entire date, use this form: I was born on December 27, 2002.

8. Don't use symbols & abbrev. in formal writing.

   Don't use symbols and abbreviations in formal writing.

9. Wow! SUPER DOOPER g!o!l!l!y! The chapter is over!!

   A bit too much emphasis, and a bit too silly, don't you think? Wow! Super dooper golly. The chapter is over!

Chapter 3

Agreement

I think we can agree that agreement is a good thing. Kids agreeing with their parents, boys agreeing with girls, teachers agreeing with students, verbs agreeing with subjects, pronouns agreeing with antecedents—these are good things. I'm sure you don't have a bit of trouble telling whether your parents agree with you about raising your allowance, but can you tell when a verb agrees with its subject? This is tricky territory, so read carefully. When you can consistently tell the difference between grammatical agreement and disagreement, your writing will soar to new heights.

Agreement Between Subject and Verb

What does agreement mean?

A singular subject needs a singular verb, and a plural subject needs a plural verb. (Reminder: The verb is the action word in the sentence. The subject is who or what does the action. See page 19 for more about verbs; see page 62 for more about subjects.)

The girl [singular subject] reads [singular verb] mystery stories.
The girls [plural subject] read [plural verb] mystery stories.

Tonya [singular subject] is [singular verb] asleep.
Tonya and her friends [plural subject] are [plural verb] asleep.

The key when figuring out whether the subject and verb agree is to find the subject of the sentence and to decide whether it's singular or plural. That's often easy. If we write "The dog eats his doggie treat," the subject (the person or thing doing the action) is the noun *dog*, and we're clearly talking about one (singular) dog. If the subject is singular, the verb needs to be singular, too. Sometimes subjects are not so easy to spot, especially when a sentence is filled with nouns. Here's a tough one: Everyone—boys, girls, their parents, their teachers, the players and their coaches—want the soccer team to go all the way to nationals. This sentence is filled with plural nouns, but the subject is *everyone*, a pronoun that means *every single one*, and it's always singular. The verb needs to be singular, too, but the verb *want* is plural. There are a number of times when it can be a little hard to figure out what the subject is, so here is a set of reminders and clues. In the following examples, <u>subjects</u> are underlined and *verbs* are italic.

Don't be confused by plural words that come after the verb.

WRONG:

My biggest <u>problem</u> *are* the many incomplete homework assignments I need to finish.

RIGHT:

My biggest <u>problem</u> *is* the many incomplete homework assignments I need to finish.

Don't be confused by plural words that come between a singular subject and the verb.

WRONG:

The <u>topic</u> of these four books *are* horses.

RIGHT:

The <u>topic</u> of these four books *is* horses.

WRONG:

<u>Each</u> of the bikes *have* new tires.

RIGHT:

<u>Each</u> of the bikes *has* new tires.

WRONG:

<u>Every one</u> of the members of both basketball teams *are* here.

RIGHT:

<u>Every one</u> of the members of both basketball teams *is* here.

Don't be confused by subjects that come at the end of the sentence.

WRONG:

Standing at the back of the room *was* my <u>parents</u>.
(Turn the sentence around and it will be clearer: My parents were standing at the back of the room.)

RIGHT:

Standing at the back of the room *were* my <u>parents</u>.

WRONG:

At the end of most of our team's games *come* victory's <u>sweetness</u>.
(Turn the sentence around: Victory's sweetness comes at the end of most of our team's games.)

RIGHT:

At the end of most of our team's games *comes* victory's <u>sweetness</u>.

Don't be confused by phrases such as *along with, together with, accompanied by, as well as, including,* and *in addition to.*

WRONG:

<u>Mila</u>, as well as Ping, *play* basketball well.

RIGHT:

<u>Mila</u>, as well as Ping, *plays* basketball well.

WRONG:

<u>Broccoli</u>, in addition to squash and all other vegetables, *are* good for you.

RIGHT:

<u>Broccoli</u>, in addition to squash and all other vegetables, *is* good for you.

Don't be confused by a *not* phrase.

WRONG:

<u>I</u>, not the other guys, *are* late.

RIGHT:

<u>I</u>, not the other guys, *am* late.

Don't be confused by collective nouns.

A collective noun names a group of people or things. Here are some examples: family, orchestra, group, committee, jury, crowd, herd, audience, and squad. Are these nouns singular or plural? They can be either, and you as the writer must decide. Ask yourself whether you're talking about the group as a whole or the individuals within the group.

SINGULAR:

The <u>football team</u> [the team as a whole] *wants* to win.

PLURAL:

The <u>football team</u> [each individual player] *put on* their uniforms.

SINGULAR:

The newly married <u>couple</u> [as a whole] *is* happy.

PLURAL:

A <u>couple</u> of people *were* late for the wedding.

Don't be confused by nouns of amount (weight, money, time, distance, temperature, measurements).

These are like collective nouns. Ask yourself whether you're talking about the amount as a whole or individual units.

SINGULAR:

<u>Five hundred dollars</u> *is* a lot of money.

PLURAL:

We have a problem: <u>five hundred-dollar bills</u> *are* missing.

SINGULAR:

<u>Fourteen tons</u> *is* a lot for a dump truck to haul.

PLURAL:

<u>Fourteen tons</u> of scrap metal *were* hauled from the junkyard.

SINGULAR:

<u>Three hours</u> *is* a long time to wait.

PLURAL:

<u>Three separate hours</u> on three separate days *were* needed to finish the exam.

The word *number* is weird. If you say "the number," it's singular. If you say "a number of," it's plural.

SINGULAR:

<u>The number</u> of kids here *is* surprisingly large.

PLURAL:

<u>A number</u> of kids *are* here.

Don't be confused by *either/or* and *neither/nor*.

<u>Either</u> Serena or Stephen *is* here.
(Both parts are singular, so use a singular verb.)

<u>Neither</u> the boys nor the girls *are* here.
(Both parts are plural, so use a plural verb.)

<u>Neither</u> the boys nor their mother *is* here.
(One part is plural and one part is singular. The singular part comes right before the verb, so use a singular verb.)

<u>Neither</u> the mother nor her sons *are* here.
(One part is plural and one part is singular. The plural part comes right before the verb, so use a plural verb.)

WRONG:

<u>Either</u> Annabelle or Isa *are* dancing the part of Aurora in the ballet.

RIGHT:

<u>Either</u> Annabelle or Isa *is* dancing the part of Aurora in the ballet.

Don't be confused by noun phrases referring to a single unit.

Sometimes a noun phrase sounds plural but describes something we think of as a single unit. These noun phrases take a singular verb.

<u>Spaghetti and meatballs</u> *is* my favorite dinner.
<u>Ice cream and cake</u> *is* my favorite dessert.
<u>Peanut butter and jelly</u> *is* my favorite sandwich.

BUT:

<u>Broccoli and spinach</u> *are* my favorite vegetables.
(We don't think of broccoli and spinach as parts of a single unit.)

Don't be confused by nouns that look plural (they end in an *s*) but are actually singular.

The <u>news</u> *is* bad.
<u>Measles</u> *is* contagious.
<u>Mumps</u> *is* contagious, too.
<u>Checkers</u> *is* my favorite game.

Don't be confused by some *-ics* nouns that can be either singular or plural.

SINGULAR:

<u>Politics</u> *is* an interesting career.

PLURAL:

The <u>politics</u> in the presidential campaign *were* mighty dirty.

SINGULAR:

<u>Statistics</u> *is* my most interesting class.

PLURAL:

The <u>statistics</u> of the game *are* not good for our team.

Don't be confused by the plural forms of foreign words.

WRONG:

The <u>data</u> *shows* that boys watch more sports on TV than girls watch.

RIGHT:

The <u>data</u> [plural of *datum*] *show* that boys watch more sports on TV than girls watch.

(See page 9 for more about the plural forms of foreign words.)

Don't be confused by mathematical phrases.

WRONG:

<u>One and one</u> *are* two.
(If you were talking about one dog and one cat, you would use *are*. In this case, "one and one" is an idea or concept, not two separate numbers standing side by side.)

RIGHT:

<u>One and one</u> *is* two.

WRONG:

<u>Five times six</u> *are* thirty.
("Five times six" is an idea. Have you ever seen a five go up and times a six?)

RIGHT:

Five times six *is* thirty.

Don't be confused by indefinite pronouns.

I and *you* refer to specific people. There are many pronouns that refer to non-specific people—for example, nobody, somebody, anybody, and everybody. Who are those people? They are non-specific (or indefinite) because we are not referring to them as specific people or calling them by their names.

Some of the indefinite pronouns are always singular:

Any pronouns: anything, anybody, anyone
No pronouns: nothing, nobody, no one
Every pronouns: everything, everybody, everyone
Some pronouns: something, somebody, someone
Others: each, every, another, little, much, either, neither

If you examine each of these pronouns, you'll see that they all refer to one person or thing. Even the word *everybody* means every single individual person. Think of *everybody* meaning the same thing as *everyone*. All of these pronouns, when used as the subject of a sentence, need a singular verb.

Little *is* happening because nobody *has* any good dancing music.
Every lion and tiger and bear in the zoo *is* hungry.
The roller coaster ride is finished; another *costs* $5.00.

Some of the indefinite pronouns are always plural: both, others, several, few, many. If you examine each of these pronouns, you'll see that they all refer to more than one person. *Both* means there are two people or things, *several* means there are more than two, etc. Each of these pronouns needs a plural verb.

The Martin girls are twins. Both *are* here.
I like possums. Several *live* in the woods behind my house.
Some of the puppies *are* frisky and others *are* lazy.

Just to confuse us poor writers, some indefinite pronouns can be either singular or plural. The rest of the sentence tells us whether to use a singular verb or a plural verb. Here are some of these tricky pronouns: any, more, some, enough, all, most, half, none.

All of the cake *is* gone. [*Cake* is singular; use a singular verb.]

<u>All</u> of the boys *are* gone. [*Boys* is plural; use a plural verb.]

<u>Most</u> of the pie *was* eaten. [singular]
<u>Most</u> of the hot dogs *were* eaten. [plural]

<u>None</u> of the snow *has* melted. [singular]
<u>None</u> of the ice cubes *have* melted. [plural]

BRAIN TICKLERS   Set # 13

Find the goofs in these sentences and correct them.

1. The family live on Elm Street.

2. The orchestra tunes its instruments.

3. My pair of shoes are lost.

4. Every one of the boys on both the soccer team and the basketball team are psyched for the spring season.

5. One of the twins are absent today.

6. The company Video Games Galore are holding their annual picnic on Thursday.

7. Are either of my sneakers in your locker? I've lost one.

8. Macaroni and cheese are Emily's favorite do-it-yourself dinner.

9. The only problem we 500 campers have are the hundreds of wasps swarming around our ten campsites.

10. Standing there looking happy was Emma and Siena.

11. Only one out of four kids in America eat a healthy diet.

12. I can't find my catcher's glove; I hope either David or the Joneses has it.

13. Tennis, as well as cycling and swimming, are great aerobic sports.

14. Bobby, not I, want to be finished with these exercises.

15. Neither of the flowers are bright red.

16. Twenty plus six are 26.

(Answers are on pages 145–147.)

Agreement Between Pronouns and Antecedents

(Reminder: An antecedent is the noun that a pronoun stands for. See page 13 for more about pronouns and antecedents.)

A pronoun must agree with its antecedent in gender (male or female).

Not many people make this goof:

WRONG:

Each of the girls puts his stuff into the car.

RIGHT:

Each of the girls puts her stuff into the car.

A pronoun must agree with its antecedent in person.

First person (the person talking): I, we
Second person (the person I'm talking to): you
Third person (the person or thing I'm talking about): she, he, it, they

WRONG:

If students refuse to learn how to write well, you can forget a good grade in language arts.
(*You* is a pronoun; *students* is the noun it stands for. *Students* is someone the writer is talking about, so it's third person; *you* is second person.)

RIGHT:

If students [third person] refuse to learn how to write well, they [third person] can forget a good grade in language arts.

WRONG:

If people want to stay healthy, you must eat well and watch your waistline.
(*People* is third person; *you* and *your* are second person.)

STILL WRONG:

If people want to stay healthy, they must eat well and watch their waistline.
(*Waistline* is singular. Do they really have just one waistline?)

RIGHT:

If people want to stay healthy, they must eat well and watch their waistlines.

A pronoun must agree with its antecedent in number (singular or plural).

WRONG:

Each girl wants to look beautiful on their prom night.
(*Girl* is singular; *their* is plural.)

RIGHT:

Each girl wants to look beautiful on her prom night.

A boy/girl thing

OFTEN USED BUT WRONG:

If anybody is late, they'll get in trouble.
(*Anybody* is singular; *they* is plural.)

RISKY:

If anybody is late, he'll get in trouble.
(Many people feel it's sexist always to use *he*.)

BETTER:

If anybody is late, he or she will get in trouble.
(This is grammatically correct but awkward.)

EVEN BETTER:

Anyone who is late will get in trouble.

Until recently, writers always used *he* to mean "an unnamed, unspecified person." Is it fair to always use *he*? What about us girls?

PROBLEM:

Everyone wants to eat their dessert before dinner.
(This is becoming acceptable in everyday speech and writing, but it is technically wrong. I wouldn't recommend using it in formal writing.)

SOLUTION #1:

Everyone wants to eat her dessert before dinner.
(Throughout a paper, you can alternate, sometimes using *he* and sometimes using *she*. You'll often see this in books, but it can be confusing to your reader.)

SOLUTION #2:

Everyone wants to eat his/her dessert before dinner.
(Repeatedly using *his/her*, *he/she*, or *s/he* gets tedious for the reader.)

SOLUTION #3:

All the kids want to eat their dessert before dinner.
(Make the subject plural by rewriting the sentence so you can correctly use the nonsexist *they*.)

Watching out for *there's* and *there is*

Does this sound good to you?

There's only three things I need in life: chocolate, chocolate, and chocolate.

Yes, it sounds great—the chocolate, that is. The sentence, however, is wrong.

RIGHT:

There are only three things I need in life: chocolate, chocolate, and chocolate.

There's is a contraction: there is = there's. This word slips into speech and writing like a sneaky fox. Be alert. At least make it agree; at best, ax it.

WRONG:

There's a lot of things we need to discuss before I give you a raise in your allowance.

RIGHT:

There are a lot of things we need to discuss before I give you a raise in your allowance.

BETTER:

We need to discuss a lot of things before I give you a raise in your allowance.

Here are two other troublemakers that work this way: *here's* and *where's*.

WRONG:

Here's a lot of old toys and clothes you need to go through and decide what to give away.

RIGHT:

Here are a lot of old toys and clothes you need to go through and decide what to give away.

WRONG:

Where's all those monsters you said live under your bed?

RIGHT:

Where are all those monsters you said live under your bed?

BRAIN TICKLERS   Set # 14

Find the goofs in these sentences and correct them.

1.   Almost everyone likes watching fireworks on the Fourth of July, don't they?

2.   Everybody loves their mother.

3.   Wait a minute, Miranda. It's very cold outside. Here's your coat and hat.

4.   I see Laney and Phoebe, but where's the other kids?

5.   Every player on the team played their best.

6.   During the scary part of the movie, we could all feel a lot of fear rushing through our body.

7.   I don't like these kind of movies.

8.   There's a lot of good reasons to learn the rules of proper writing.

9.   All the girls wore a dress to the dance.

(Answers are on pages 148–149.)

BRAIN TICKLERS—THE ANSWERS

Set # 13, page 140

1. The family live on Elm Street.

   In order to tell whether a subject agrees with its verb, always begin by finding the subject. The subject of this sentence is *family*. It's a collective noun and can be singular or plural. In this case we are clearly talking about the family as a whole, as a single unit. It should be this: The family lives on Elm Street.

2. The orchestra tunes its instruments.

   What is the subject? *Orchestra*, and it is also a collective noun that can be singular or plural. Each individual musician tunes his or her instrument, so in this case *orchestra* is plural.

   RIGHT BUT SOUNDS WEIRD:
   The orchestra tune their instruments.

   BETTER:
   The musicians in the orchestra tune their instruments.

3. My pair of shoes are lost.

   What is the subject? It might sound like *shoes* is the subject, but it is not. The subject is *pair*. The word *pair*, even though it means two of something, is very often a singular noun. (Yes, English is sometimes a very wacky language.) Both of these are correct:
   • My pair of shoes is lost.
   • My shoes are lost.

4. Every one of the boys on both the soccer team and the basketball team are psyched for the spring season.

   The subject of the sentence is not *boys* (which is plural) but *every one* (which is singular). We are talking about each separate boy, each and every <u>one</u>, not the whole bunch of boys as a group. The pronoun *one* is always a clue that the subject is singular. This is correct: Every one of the boys on both the soccer team and the basketball team <u>is</u> psyched for the spring season.

5. One of the twins are absent today.

   What is the subject? It is *one*, not twins. The pronoun *one* is always singular. That makes sense, doesn't it? Even if we're talking about one of the zillion mosquitos flying around, we're still talking about just one, and that one is singular. This is correct: One of the twins <u>is</u> absent today.

6. The company Video Games Galore are holding their annual picnic on Thursday.

   What is the subject? It is *company*. A company is composed of lots of people, but in this case we're talking about the company as a whole. When a group of people come together to have a picnic, they are functioning as one group, and that one is singular. The company Video Games Galore <u>is</u> holding <u>its</u> annual picnic on Thursday.

7. Are either of my sneakers in your locker? I've lost one.

   What is the subject? It is *either*, a pronoun that implies there are two things (or people) and we are asking about one of them. That one is singular. <u>Is</u> either of my sneakers in your locker?

8. Macaroni and cheese are Emily's favorite do-it-yourself dinner.

   The subject is *macaroni and cheese*. Does Emily like macaroni, broccoli, tomatoes, and cheese? No, she likes macaroniandcheese, that dish that we think of as almost one word. Those sorts of words we treat as singular. Macaroni and cheese <u>is</u> Emily's favorite do-it-yourself dinner.

9. The only problem we 500 campers have are the hundreds of wasps swarming around our ten campsites.

   What is the subject? This sentence is filled with plural nouns (campers, wasps, campsites), but none of those is the subject. The subject is *the only problem*, or more specifically, the noun *problem*. The phrase *the only problem* gives us a hint that this will need a singular verb because we are talking about only one problem. This is correct: The only problem we 500 campers have <u>is</u> the hundreds of wasps swarming around our ten campsites.

10. Standing there looking happy was Emma and Siena.

    What is the subject? In this case the subject doesn't appear until the end of the sentence. *Emma and Siena* is the subject. There are two girls, and that tells us we need a plural verb. Standing there looking happy <u>were</u> Emma and Siena. Notice if you turn this sentence around, the choice of a verb is clear: Emma and Siena <u>were</u> standing there looking happy.

11. Only one out of four kids in America eat a healthy diet.

    This is a sad statement about our times, but that's not our concern here. What we need to know is, what's the subject? *One* is the subject and it's singular. Only one out of four kids in America <u>eats</u> a healthy diet.

12. I can't find my catcher's glove; I hope either David or the Joneses has it.

    The Joneses comes closer to the verb. It's plural, so a plural verb is needed. I can't find my catcher's glove; I hope either David or the Joneses <u>have</u> it.

13. Tennis, as well as cycling and swimming, are great aerobic sports.

    The subject of the sentence is *tennis*, and it is singular. Don't be confused by *as well as* and similar phrases. Tennis, as well as cycling and swimming, <u>is</u> a great aerobic sport.

14. Bobby, not I, want to be finished with these exercises.

    Bobby is the singular subject of the sentence. Bobby, not I, <u>wants</u> to be finished with these exercises.

15. Neither of the flowers are bright red.

    What is the subject? It is the pronoun *neither*, which means *not this one and not that one*. It's a word about ones, implying that it is singular. Be alert for this very common goof; the word *neither* is very often used incorrectly as if it were plural. This is correct: Neither of the flowers <u>is</u> bright red.

16. Twenty plus six are 26.

    What is the subject? It is *twenty plus six*, and that's certainly more than one. However, we're not talking about 26 individual numbers marching around on your math book; we're talking about an idea, and ideas are singular. Twenty plus six <u>is</u> 26.

Set # 14, page 144

1. Almost everyone likes watching fireworks on the Fourth of July, don't they?

   This is how we often speak, but it's not how we write. *Everyone* is singular, *they* is plural. Both of these are correct:

   - Almost everyone likes watching fireworks on the Fourth of July, right?
   - Almost all people like watching fireworks on the Fourth of July, don't they?

2. Everybody loves their mother.

   Everybody is singular, *their* is plural, *mother* is singular. Here are two possible solutions:
   - Everybody loves his or her mother.
   - People love their mothers.

3. Wait a minute, Miranda. It's very cold outside. Here's your coat and hat.

   Here *is* your coat and hat? That won't fly. It should be this: Here <u>are</u> your coat and hat.

4. I see Laney and Phoebe, but where's the other kids?

   Where *is* the other kids? I see Laney and Phoebe, but where <u>are</u> the other kids?

5. Every player on the team played their best.

   Every is singular, *their* is plural. Here are two solutions:
   - Every player on the team played his/her best.
   - All the players on the team played their best.

6. During the scary part of the movie, we could all feel a lot of fear rushing through our body.

   How many people share this one body? During the scary part of the movie, we could all feel a lot of fear rushing through our <u>bodies</u>.

7. I don't like these kind of movies.

    These is plural, *kind* is singular, and *movies* is plural. Both of these are correct:
    *   I don't like <u>this</u> <u>kind</u> of <u>movie</u>. (All three underlined words are singular.)
    *   I don't like <u>these</u> <u>kinds</u> of <u>movies</u>. (All three underlined words are plural.)

8. There's a lot of good reasons to learn the rules of proper writing.

    Now there's some bad writing! There <u>are</u> a lot of good reasons to learn the rules of proper writing.

9. All the girls wore a dress to the dance.

    That must have been one huge dress! I bet you mean this: All the girls wore <u>dresses</u> to the dance.

Chapter 4

Words, Words, Words

Wacky Words We Love to Misuse

Read this paragraph aloud: I am sure that everyone of you all ready knows that spoken English and written English are sometimes very different than each other. What sounds fine to the ear sometimes looks weak, informal, or even dumb on paper. For example, we say "I should of eaten my veggies," but what we are suppose to write is this: "I should *have* eaten my veggies." We are so use to seeing and hearing certain words and phrases misused that we often don't even notice them when we proofread our papers. However, if you plan on getting *A*'s on alot of your language arts papers, you better learn to spot these sorts of goofs. What are these sneaky, wacky words? Read on! I insure you that if you read this chapter, you will discover that their are quite a few words which you are misusing.

Did that paragraph sound fine to you? It probably did, but it was filled with wacky words—words we often use in speech and writing that are wrong. How many of these wacky words did you catch in that paragraph?

This	should be this
everyone of you	every one of you
all ready knows	already knows
different than each other	different from each other
suppose to write	supposed to write
use to seeing	used to seeing
plan on getting A's	plan to get A's
alot	a lot
you better learn	you had better learn
I insure you	I assure you
their are	there are
which you are misusing	that you are misusing

A and An

Use *a* before words beginning with consonant sounds, even if that sound is made by a vowel. (Reminder: consonants are all the letters of the alphabet except *a, e, i, o, u,* and sometimes *y.*)

a bat	a hat	a cat
a university	a yo-yo	a 100-dollar bill

Use *an* before words beginning with vowel sounds, even if that sound is made by a consonant. (Reminder: the vowels are *a, e, i, o, u,* and sometimes *y.*)

an oasis	an M&M	an honor (silent *h*)
an apple	an *F*	an hour (silent *h*)

Affect and Effect

These are two tricky words! Here is the key to using them correctly:

EFFECT:

As a noun = the result or outcome of something
If you don't wear your bicycle helmet, the <u>effect</u> could be very bad.
As a verb = to cause or to make something happen
The teacher tried to <u>effect</u> a change in the students' study habits.

AFFECT:

As a noun = emotions (a rarely used word except by psychologists)
The child's <u>affect</u> was disturbed after she saw the scary movie.
As a verb = to influence something
The movie didn't <u>affect</u> me as much as it did my little sister.

If it's a noun you need, almost always choose *effect.*

Scary movies have a bad <u>effect</u> on many kids.
My apology didn't have the <u>effect</u> I thought it would have.

If it's a verb you need, almost always choose *affect.*

Too much rainy weather <u>affects</u> my mood; it makes me grumpy.

All Right and Alright

VERY IFFY:

Is it <u>alright</u> to write this way?

VERY SAFE:

Is it all right to write this way?

Many teachers and writers will tell you that *alright* is not a word and is never acceptable. My computer spellchecker gasps in horror every time I type *alright*. However, some dictionaries say it is slowly gaining a tiny bit of acceptance. In formal writing, don't trust that tiny bit of acceptance because most people will think you've made a major goof. A hundred years from now it may be all right to use *alright* in formal writing, but right now it is not.

Almost and Most

Students often use *most* when *almost* is much better.

INFORMAL:

Most everybody we invited showed up for the party.

BETTER:

Almost everybody we invited showed up for the party.

A lot and [Alot]

There is no such word as *alot*.

WRONG:

This is a goof that writers make alot.

RIGHT:

This is a goof that writers make a lot.

Among and Between

Use *between* when there are two people or things involved; use *among* when there are more than two involved.

RIGHT:

This is just between Laura and me.

RIGHT:

Among the three girls, Jamie runs the fastest.

Exception to the rule: when you're talking about differences, use *between*.

RIGHT:

Do you know the difference <u>between</u> bees, wasps, and hornets?

Amount and Number

Amount = how much (you can't count them)
Number = how many (you can count them)

WRONG:

A large <u>amount</u> <u>of</u> <u>kids</u> were absent from school today.

RIGHT:

A large <u>number</u> <u>of</u> <u>kids</u> were absent from school today because a large <u>amount</u> <u>of</u> <u>snow</u> fell during the night.

And and To

Students often use the word *and* when the better word is *to*.

INFORMAL:

When you write papers, <u>try</u> <u>and</u> write right.

FORMAL:

When you write papers, <u>try</u> <u>to</u> write right.

INFORMAL:

Be <u>sure</u> <u>and</u> study for the test.

FORMAL:

Be <u>sure</u> <u>to</u> study for the test.

Around and About

It is not absolutely wrong to use *around* to mean *approximately*, but it is very informal.

INFORMAL:

I am a heavyweight wrestler, and I weigh <u>around</u> 240.

FORMAL:

I am a heavyweight wrestler. I weigh <u>about</u> 240 and I run <u>around</u> the house twenty times every night before bedtime.

BRAIN TICKLERS   Set # 15

Find the goofs in these sentences and correct them.

1.   My sister is going to an university in Wyoming.

2.   I don't like the affect that movie had on Leslie; she's worn her rhinestone tiara and her boa shawl to school every day for the past week.

3.   I used to do alright in math, but recently I don't like it alot.

4.   Most all the kids on the tennis team are in eighth grade.

5.   Who is the best gymnast between the three boys?

6.   Please give me a large amount of apples.

7.   I am around five feet tall.

8.   Try and be here by noon.

(Answers are on page 176.)

REMINDER

Spoken English and written English (at least properly written formal English) are sometimes very different. Unless you are deliberately writing in a chatty, casual style, check your writing carefully for signs of informal English. Don't worry about how you sound. Formal English doesn't sound stuffy and weird—it sounds clear, clean, and strong.

Behind and In back of

In back of is very informal.

INFORMAL:

Bonnie, put your bicycle <u>in back of</u> the house.

BETTER:

Bonnie, put your bicycle <u>behind</u> the house.

Bring and Take

Bring shows movement toward the speaker.
Take shows movement away from the speaker.

WRONG:

As I ran out the door, Dad shouted, "Here, remember to <u>bring</u> your lunch with you to school."

RIGHT:

As I ran out the door, Dad shouted, "Here, remember to <u>take</u> your lunch with you to school, and <u>bring</u> home your empty lunch box."

Can and May

Can = has the ability to do something
May = has permission to do something
May = might do something

INFORMAL:

<u>Can</u> I have a hamburger, please?

BETTER:

<u>May</u> I have a hamburger, please?

RIGHT:

Jake <u>can</u> play baseball well. (He has the ability.)

RIGHT:

Hartley <u>may</u> play baseball this spring, but he hasn't decided yet. (He might play baseball.)

RIGHT:

Lucas <u>may</u> not play baseball until he has done his homework. (He does not have permission.)

Capital and Capitol

Be careful with the spelling of these two sound-alike words (homonyms). The word *capital* can mean several different things, but the word *capitol* is always a building. Here's a way to remember the difference: capitol buildings usually have domes on the top, and the letter *o* looks a little like a dome.

Austin is the <u>capital</u> city of Texas, and Austin begins with a <u>capital</u> letter. The building where the Texas legislature meets is the <u>capitol</u>.

Dessert and Desert

A <u>desert</u> is a hot, dry, sandy place; a <u>dessert</u> is a sweet reward for eating all your vegetables at dinner.

I want chocolate cream pie for <u>dessert</u>.
Those poor nomads riding their camels through the <u>desert</u> probably haven't had a bite of chocolate cream pie in months.

Different from and Different than

Different from is better when you're comparing two things, but *different than* is better when a clause follows.

(A clause is a group of words that contains a subject and a verb. See page 63 for more about clauses.)

COMPARISON:

Your shoes are different <u>from</u> mine.

WITH A CLAUSE:

This movie is different <u>than</u> I thought it would be.

Every place and Everywhere

These are very informal: *every place, some place, any place, no place.*

INFORMAL:

I've looked <u>every</u> <u>place</u> for my social studies book. There's <u>no</u> <u>place</u> left to look, but it must be <u>some</u> <u>place</u> around here.

BETTER:

I've looked <u>everywhere</u> for my social studies book. There's <u>nowhere</u> left to look, but it must be <u>somewhere</u> around here.

Farther and Further

Use *farther* and *farthest* for distance.

I'm too tired to walk <u>farther</u>.
Hazel lives <u>farther</u> from my house than I thought.

Use *further* and *furthest* to mean longer or more.

I want to study this <u>further</u>. (meaning longer or in more depth)
This conversation can go no <u>further</u>. (meaning no longer)

Fewer and Less

If you can count them, use *fewer*. If you can't count them, use *less*.

There has been <u>less</u> snow this year than last year, so we have <u>fewer</u> snow days to make up. (You can't count snow; you can count days.)
We have <u>less</u> milk, <u>less</u> butter, <u>fewer</u> grapes, <u>less</u> maple syrup, and <u>fewer</u> potatoes in our refrigerator than you have in yours.

Foot and Feet

Many people use *foot* when *feet* is correct.

WRONG:

The swimming pool is twelve <u>foot</u> deep.

RIGHT:

The swimming pool is twelve <u>feet</u> deep.

WRONG:

The lifeguard is six <u>foot</u> tall.

RIGHT:

The lifeguard is six <u>feet</u> tall.

It is correct to use *foot* in compound adjectives (two-word adjectives) that come before the noun that they describe.

I need four <u>10-foot</u> boards of treated lumber.
We have two <u>7-foot</u> players on our basketball team.

BRAIN TICKLERS   Set # 16

Find the goofs in these sentences and correct them.

1. Less people live in Canada than in the United States.

2. Can I eat now?

3. When I was at Grandma's house, she said, "Here's one of my famous baked hams. Bring it to your mom."

4. I'd like to go someplace really fun on our date tonight.

5. My science project is very different than Lydia's.

6. I'm exhausted. I don't think I can swim one inch further.

7. The doctor says that, judging by my shoe size, I should be about six foot tall when I finish growing.

8. The bag of chips fell down in back of the refrigerator.

(Answers are on page 177.)

Good and Well

Good is an adjective and *well* is an adverb.

If you remember that, you have the *good/well* problem licked.

Old Blue is a <u>good</u> dog. (adjective describing the noun *dog*)
You trained Old Blue <u>well</u>. (adverb describing the verb *trained*)
This is a <u>good</u> salad. (adjective describing the noun *salad*)
I can't taste the salad <u>well</u> because I have a cold. (adverb describing the verb *taste*)

Remember linking verbs and action verbs? (See page 38.)

You <u>smell</u> <u>good</u>; that's a nice perfume. (*smell* is a linking verb)
Now that you took your cold medicine, you should be able to <u>smell</u> <u>well</u>. (*smell* is an action verb)
You <u>look</u> <u>good</u>. (*look* is a linking verb)
<u>Look</u> at this picture <u>well</u>. (*look* is an action verb)

Which is correct?

I'm over my cold and I feel <u>well</u>.
I'm over my cold and I feel <u>good</u>.

Both are correct. It is okay to use *well* as an adjective when you're talking about health.

Have and Got

Notice how often you can get rid of the word *got*. Saying "I have got" is kind of silly, if you think about it, because "I have" says it all.

INFORMAL:

I haven't got enough money to buy the pet python I want.

BETTER:

I don't have enough money to buy the pet python I want.

INFORMAL:

I have really got to study these wacky words for the wacky test tomorrow.

BETTER:

I really have to study these wacky words for the wacky test tomorrow.

Have and Of

The word *of* is often used when *have* is the correct word.

WRONG:

If he would of listened to me, this never would of happened.

RIGHT:

If he would have listened to me, this never would have happened.

WRONG:

I could of run that race faster. I should of tried harder.

RIGHT:

I could have run that race faster. I should have tried harder.

WRONG:

Tori might of made the highest grade in the class.

RIGHT:

Tori might have made the highest grade in the class.

How and That

How is often used as a conjunction when the correct word is *that*.

INFORMAL:

Stop reminding me <u>how</u> I have more homework to do.

BETTER:

Stop reminding me <u>that</u> I have more homework to do.

INFORMAL:

Trent is complaining <u>how</u> there's not enough peach pie for him to have another piece.

BETTER:

Trent is complaining <u>that</u> there's not enough peach pie for him to have another piece.

In and Into

In indicates where something is right now.

Into implies movement from one place to another.

INFORMAL:

Put the ice cream <u>in</u> the freezer.

BETTER:

Put the ice cream <u>into</u> the freezer.

RIGHT:

Mom yelled, "I am <u>in</u> the car waiting for you. If you don't get <u>into</u> the car right now, you're going to see tire tracks."

Its and It's

Confusing the words *its* and *it's* is one of the most common mistakes in the English language. We see this goof everywhere! Two such little words, yet they cause such big trouble.

The word *it's* is short for either *it is* or *it has*. It never means anything else, and it never shows possession.

WRONG:

<u>Its</u> absolutely amazing how often students make this mistake.

RIGHT:

<u>It's</u> even more amazing how often adults make this mistake!

If it's Bill's banjo, Sofia's sofa, and Jesse's giraffe, why is the giraffe's tail not *it's* tail? you might ask. That's an excellent question, and the only answer I can give you is "just because." This is one of those odd times when what makes absolutely good sense (the giraffe's tail = it's tail) is absolutely wrong. Possessive nouns (the cat's meow) take apostrophes; possessive pronouns (its, his, hers, my, ours, theirs, yours) *never never never* take apostrophes.

We don't make the apostrophe mistake with most of these pronouns. If someone wrote about his's name, my's cell phone, your's house, and their's computer, we would laugh and think, oh how silly. But when someone writes that its time to give the dog it's bath, we barely notice that there are two very serious apostrophe mistakes in the sentence.

The other possessive pronoun that sometimes can give writers trouble is *whose*. Students often confuse *who's* with *whose*. The word *who's* means only two things: *who is* or *who has*. This sentence is correct: <u>Who's</u> been wearing my T-shirt and <u>whose</u> T-shirt is this I've been wearing by mistake?

Irregardless and Regardless

Most dictionaries say *irregardless* is not a word. It is used all the time, but it is considered either downright wrong or at least a "nonstandard" word. The correct form of this word is *regardless*. (Another example of a "nonstandard" word would be *ain't*. We hear it used and see it written often, but in formal writing it would be considered incorrect.)

WRONG:

You should use words correctly <u>irregardless</u> of how other people use them.

RIGHT:

<u>Regardless</u> of how often you hear people say *irregardless*, you're better off never using that word, and *regardless* is shorter to write or say anyway.

There are many ways that we say *NO!* in the English language. We often do it by putting a prefix in front of a word. And there are a lot of them that we use. Check these out:

likely—<u>un</u>likely
complete—<u>in</u>complete
modest—<u>im</u>modest
reversible—<u>ir</u>reversible
logical—<u>il</u>logical
understood—<u>mis</u>understood

It would seem that *irregardless* is the *NO!* form of *regardless*, but it's not. They mean exactly the same thing. Isn't that weird?

There's one other pair of wacky words that works that way in our language. The word *inflammable* means exactly the same thing as *flammable*. Always go for the simplest, shortest option; in this case that would be *flammable*.

Like

SAY WHAT?

I was like wow when you said you were coming and then like so down when you couldn't.

The word *like* is used these days to mean many things that it doesn't actually mean.

LIKE, MEANING "TO SAY":

I was like no.

LIKE, MEANING "TO FEEL":

I was like bummed.

LIKE, MEANING "UMMMM":

I was very sorry to like miss the party because I really like wanted to be there.

LIKE, MEANING "VERY" OR "REALLY":

She's like gorgeous.

When words in our language take on new, different, or special meanings, they are called "slang" words. If people use them long enough, they become accepted parts of our language. Usually, however, they die out in a few years. When your children are your age, they may have no idea what "like wow" means. They'll have created their own slang! There's nothing wrong with slang—our language would be very stuffy and boring without it—but be aware that it's very weak in formal writing or speaking.

Look at all the ways *like* can be used correctly:

VERB:

I like spinach.

NOUN:

You understand my food likes and dislikes.

PREPOSITION:

I love green, leafy veggies like spinach.

ADJECTIVE:

We seem to be of like minds about green, leafy things.

ADVERB:

You likely enjoy collard greens, too, right?

CONJUNCTION:

It looks like I could turn into the Jolly Green Giant if I keep eating this way!

Like is used as a preposition when we're comparing one thing to another.

You look like your mother.
This soda does not taste like that one.

Sometimes comparisons are two separate clauses and a conjunction is needed. To use *like* as a conjunction is okay in informal writing, but in formal writing, it's better to use *as though* or *as if*.

INFORMAL:

You look like you've seen a ghost.

FORMAL:

You look as if you've seen a ghost.

INFORMAL:

Charlie ran like he had rockets on his shoes.

FORMAL:

Charlie ran as though he had rockets on his shoes.

Me and Myself

Some people think that saying *myself* sounds more polite than saying *me* or *I*. It doesn't—it just sounds wrong. Never use *myself* when *me* or *I* sounds right. (The same goes for *yourself*, *herself*, and *himself*.)

WRONG:

Kristen and <u>myself</u> were invited to the party.

RIGHT:

Kristen and <u>I</u> were invited to the party.

WRONG:

Mom baked chocolate chip cookies for Molly and <u>myself</u>.

RIGHT:

Mom baked chocolate chip cookies for Molly and <u>me</u>.

When is *myself* correct? See page 12.

BRAIN TICKLERS   Set # 17

Find the goofs in these sentences and correct them.

1. Don't throw anything in the shark tank.

2. I would of gotten you a present if I'd known it's your birthday.

3. Did I do good on that last exercise?

4. I was like no way when my brother tried to get me to eat some raw hamburger.

5. Have you got any cash on you?

6. I've been thinking lately how I'd like to learn to play a musical instrument.

7. Sawyer and myself really appreciate your giving us a ride.

8. Good job! You skied very good today.

9. This is the end of this set of exercises. Its finished!

(Answers are on pages 178–179.)

Passed and Past

These two sound-alike words (homonyms) are often mixed up. The word *passed* is the past tense of the verb to *pass*.

I <u>passed</u> the football to Joaquin.
The time <u>passed</u> slowly.
I <u>passed</u> my math exam with flying colors!

The word *past* tells us where something is located in time or in space.

In the <u>past</u>, people traveled in horse-drawn carriages.
The era of horse-drawn carriages is long <u>past</u>.
My house is the one just <u>past</u> the elementary school.

Plan on and Plan to

Plan on is very informal.

INFORMAL:

Do you <u>plan on going</u> to the football game?

BETTER:

Do you <u>plan to go</u> to the football game?

Principal and Principle

A principal is usually a person. An easy way to remember this is "the princi<u>pal</u> is my <u>pal</u>." Whatever group the principal is part of, this word implies that he or she is high ranking or perhaps the top dog.

Dr. Edwards is the <u>principal</u> of our school, and Susan is a <u>principal</u> [meaning first-ranked dancer] in the ballet company.

Sometimes *principal* is a financial term.

When you borrow money from a bank, you have to pay back the <u>principal</u> [meaning the amount you borrowed] plus interest.

Sometimes *principal* means "primary or main."

The <u>principal</u> reason I made an A on the Spanish test is that I studied like crazy; of course, the fact that my mom speaks Spanish fluently and speaks it often to me didn't hurt.

A *principle* is a belief, a rule or standard of good behavior, or a law of science or nature.

A BELIEF:

The United States was founded on the <u>principles</u> of democracy.

A RULE OR STANDARD:

All religions have a strong set of <u>principles</u> regarding how we should treat our fellow man.

A LAW OF SCIENCE OR NATURE:

We are studying the <u>principle</u> of jet propulsion.

Sit and Set

Sit means "to take a seat or sit down."

I want to <u>sit</u> here a while and rest.
<u>Sit</u> in the blue chair.

Set means "to place something."

Please <u>set</u> this blue chair in that corner.
<u>Set</u> the red cushion on the blue chair.

WRONG:

Miranda, why did you <u>sit</u> your grammar book on top of a hot stove when you knew it would catch fire?

RIGHT:

Miranda, why did you <u>set</u> your grammar book on top of a hot stove when you knew it would catch fire?

WRONG:

For that, Miranda, you must <u>set</u> in the corner for an hour and think about your poor, sad grammar book.

RIGHT:

For that, Miranda, you must <u>sit</u> in the corner for an hour and think about your poor, sad grammar book.

Than and Then

Students often use the word *then* when they mean *than*.

Than is a conjunction. It links two parts of a sentence that are being compared to each other.

RIGHT:

My dog barks louder <u>than</u> your dog barks.

Then is an adverb telling when something happened.

RIGHT:

Lucy finished her book, <u>then</u> crawled into bed and fell asleep.

WRONG:

I have more homework tonight <u>then</u> you do.

RIGHT:

I have more homework tonight <u>than</u> you do.

This and A

This is a very overused word. It implies something right here, close at hand. Don't use *this* when the word *a* is better.

RIGHT:

Look at <u>this</u> splinter right here in my foot.

INFORMAL:

I bought <u>this</u> great new dress that I want to show you.

BETTER:

I bought <u>a</u> great new dress that I want to show you.

INFORMAL:

There's <u>this</u> new video game on the market that I'm dying to buy.

BETTER:

There's <u>a</u> new video game on the market that I'm dying to buy.

Which and That

That is the first word of a phrase or clause that is essential for the sentence to make sense or to mean what you want it to mean (see page 63 for more about phrases and clauses).

RIGHT:

The bike <u>that</u> I want for my birthday is a 30-speed, blue mountain bike.
(I'm not talking about just any bike; I'm talking specifically about the one I want for my birthday. The clause "that I want for my birthday" tells exactly

which bike I'm talking about. Without that clause, the sentence doesn't say what I mean.)

DOESN'T SAY WHAT I MEAN:

The bike is a 30-speed, blue mountain bike.

Which is the first word of a phrase or clause that is not essential. If you can insert the words "by the way" and the sentence still means what you want it to mean, use *which*.

RIGHT:

My blue mountain bike, which I got for my birthday, has 30 speeds.
(The clause "which I got for my birthday" is a by-the-way clause. The information is not essential—I could leave it out and the sentence would still make sense.)

DOES SAY WHAT I MEAN:

My blue mountain bike has 30 speeds.

When the information is essential, use *that* and don't use commas. When the information is not essential, use *which* and do use commas.

WRONG:

The dogs which are barking are hungry.

RIGHT:

The dogs that are barking are hungry.
("That are barking" is essential for this sentence to make sense.)

WRONG:

My left foot that is slightly bigger than my right foot is the one I broke.
(The fact that my left foot is slightly bigger than my right foot is a by-the-way phrase. This information is not necessary in order for the sentence to make sense.)

RIGHT:

My left foot, which is slightly bigger than my right foot, is the one I broke.
(Notice the two commas that appear in this sentence. Commas come before and after by-the-way phrases.)

Sometimes either *which* or *that* can be correct, but they make the sentence mean entirely different things. Check this out:

RIGHT:

Sofia's cat that I love is named Olivia.
(This is correct if Sofia has three or four cats that I don't like and one named Olivia that I do like. If that were the case, the sentence "Sofia's cat is named Olivia" doesn't say at all what I'm trying to say. The phrase *that I love* is necessary for this sentence to make sense and to point to exactly the right cat, the one that I love. When information is necessary, use *that* and no commas.)

ALSO RIGHT:

Sofia's cat, which I love, is named Olivia.
(In this case Sofia has one cat, its name is Olivia and—oh, by the way—I love it. The sentence "Sofia's cat is named Olivia" does make sense, and the extra information about my loving the cat is an interesting addition, but it is not absolutely necessary. When information is not necessary, use *which* and do use commas.)

Which and Who

Use *which* for things; use *who* for people.

WRONG:

My brother is the one <u>which</u> fed our dinner to the dog, not me!

RIGHT:

My brother is the one <u>who</u> fed our dinner to the dog, not me!

Who and Whom

Writers get so confused over *who* and *whom* that they often give up and use *who* all the time. As a result, *whom* is about to die out of our language. There's really no reason to be afraid of *who* and *whom* because the trick for remembering which to use is quite easy. When in doubt, substitute the words *he* and *him*. Notice which sounds better. If *he* is correct, use *who*. If *him* (with an *m*) is correct, use *whom* (with an *m*).

- I wonder (who/whom) will be at baseball practice today.

Which sounds okay?

- he will be at practice today—sounds okay
- him will be at practice today—does not sound okay

RIGHT:

I wonder <u>who</u> will be at baseball practice today.

- Never argue with the guy (who/whom) is wearing the umpire's suit!

Which sounds okay?

- he is wearing the suit—sounds okay
- him is wearing the suit—does not sound okay

RIGHT:

Never argue with the guy <u>who</u> is wearing the umpire's suit!

- We all wondered (who/whom) the winner was.

Which sounds okay?

- he was the winner—sounds okay
- him was the winner—does not sound okay

RIGHT:

We all wondered <u>who</u> the winner was.

- With (who/whom) are you going?

Which sounds okay?

- I'm going with he—does not sound okay
- I'm going with him—sounds okay

RIGHT:

With <u>whom</u> are you going?

- (Who/Whom) is the present for?

Which sounds okay?

- that is for he—does not sound okay
- that is for him—sounds okay

RIGHT:

Whom is the present for?
(Asking "Who's the present for?" is acceptable in everyday speech, but for formal writing, using *whom* correctly will serve you very well.)

Why, How come, and What for

How come and *what for* are very informal.

INFORMAL:

What are you doing that for?

BETTER:

Why are you doing that?

INFORMAL:

How come you're not taking the bus to school?

BETTER:

Why are you not taking the bus to school?

One Word or Two?

Many times students use one word when two words are needed.

Here's a clue for when the proper choice is two words: Can you put other words in the middle? If so, use two words.

WRONG:

We were already to leave.

RIGHT:

We were all [set and packed and] ready to leave.

WRONG:

I want pizza everyday for dinner.

RIGHT:

I want pizza every [single] day for dinner.

Each of these sentences is correct:

We were all ready to leave when we noticed that Keelie had already left.

Does <u>anyone</u> know whether <u>any one</u> of my friends is going to the dance?

<u>Sometime</u> in the future I would love to spend <u>some time</u> in Alaska.

<u>Everyone</u> knew that many kids had gone to the circus, and <u>every one</u> of them had a good time.

<u>Every day</u> I find myself getting upset by <u>everyday</u> problems like too much homework to do.

<u>Somebody</u> told the lifeguard that <u>some body</u>, probably a mouse or a rat, was floating in the swimming pool.

Confusing Pears

Which word should I use?   Which word should I write?
  or is it   or is it
Which word should I yews?   Which word should I right?
  or is it   or is it
Which word should I you's?   Which word should I rite?

It may knot seam fare, but their are dozens of confusing pears (and trios) of words in the English language, and writers often fowl up when using them. It happens all the thyme—we use won word when we mean another. We make word errors day and knight! Eye will give yew a peace of advice: Reed your work carefully and bee alert four these sneaky critters. Goodness nose, I'd be embarrassed if I rote a paper with two many goofs! Aye no ewe wood bee two, sew hears sum aide from mi too yew.

Did you catch all these goofs?

knot—not	seam—seem	fare—fair
their—there	pears—pairs	fowl—foul
thyme—time	won—one	knight—night
eye—I	yew—you	peace—piece
reed—read	bee—be	four—for
nose—knows	rote—wrote	two—too
aye—I	no—know	ewe—you
wood—would	bee—be	two—too
sew—so	hears—here's	sum—some
aide—aid	mi—me	too—to
yew—you		

Do you know when to use one word and when to use the other? Don't sweat it—even the pros often get confused. That's why the pros' favorite book (or website) is the dictionary.

Read this list, but don't try to memorize all these words. Enjoy the fun of two words masquerading as each other; words often completely change their meanings by altering only a letter or two. When you are even a bit unsure about the precise meaning of a word, look it up.

SOME FREQUENTLY MIXED-UP WORDS

accept—except	envelope—envelop
advice—advise	forward—foreword
alter—altar	human—humane
assure—ensure—insure	hurdle—hurtle
bait—bate	intense—intensive
born—borne	later—latter
breath—breathe	moral—morale
clinch—clench	personal—personnel
compliment—complement	prophecy—prophesy
confident—confidant	stationery—stationary
emigrate—immigrate	track—tract
eminent—imminent	yea—yeah

BRAIN TICKLERS   Set # 18

Find the goofs in these sentences and correct them.

1. The nervous hikers past a large, fresh pile of what looked suspiciously like bear scat.

2. Do you plan on updating your sports blog today?

3. Sit your luggage down and come set for a few minutes.

4. Did every one on the football team pass everyone of his final exams?

5. Joe is the chef whom cooked that fabulous stir fry.

6. Jasmin is one of my friends which live in India.

7. My nose that has been stuffy all spring would appreciate a reduction in the pollen in the air.

8. Francine has lost more weight then Abigail.

9. This is a long reign.

10. What did you bring your racket for? It's snowing.

11. I had this puppy when I was younger with a cute black patch on his left eye.

12. The grocery store which carries my favorite granola is the Trader Joe's on Main Street.

13. Who did you give your outgrown tutu to?

14. Its knot save two-holed you're breathe four two lounge.

(Answers are on pages 179–181.)

BRAIN TICKLERS—THE ANSWERS

Set # 15, page 155

1. My sister is going to an university in Wyoming.

   Even though *u* is a vowel, in this case it makes a consonant sound. My sister is going to <u>a</u> university in Wyoming.

2. I don't like the affect that movie had on Leslie; she's worn her rhinestone tiara and her boa shawl to school every day for the past week.

   If it's a noun you need, usually use *effect*. I don't like the <u>effect</u> [meaning the result or outcome] that movie had on Leslie.

3. I used to do alright in math, but recently I don't like it alot.

   Alright is a very iffy word and *alot* is not a word at all. I used to do <u>all</u> <u>right</u> in math, but recently I don't like it a lot.

4. Most all the kids on the tennis team are in eighth grade.

   Most all is very informal. This is better: <u>Almost</u> all the kids on the tennis team are in eighth grade.

5. Who is the best gymnast between the three boys?

   There are three boys involved. Who is the best gymnast <u>among</u> the three boys?

6. Please give me a large amount of apples.

   You can count apples, so use *number*, not *amount*. Please give me a large <u>number</u> of apples.

7. I am around five feet tall.

   This sentence is very informal. This is better: I am <u>about</u> five feet tall.

8. Try and be here by noon.

   Very informal. To be more formal, this is better: Try <u>to</u> be here by noon.

Set # 16, page 159

1. Less people live in Canada than in the United States.

    You can count people, so use *fewer*, not *less*. <u>Fewer</u> people live in Canada than in the United States.

2. Can I eat now?

    Are you asking whether you have the ability or the permission? I assume you *can* eat now, unless your jaw is wired shut. If it's permission you're asking for, this is correct: <u>May</u> I eat now?

3. When I was at Grandma's house, she said, "Here's one of my famous baked hams. Bring it to your mom."

    Bring implies something coming toward the speaker. What Grandma meant to say was, "Here's one of my famous baked hams. <u>Take</u> it to your mom."

4. I'd like to go someplace really fun on our date tonight.

    The word *someplace* is very informal. This is better: I'd like to go <u>somewhere</u> really fun on our date tonight.

5. My science project is very different than Lydia's.

    When you're comparing two things, use *different from*. My science project is very different <u>from</u> Lydia's.

6. I'm exhausted. I don't think I can swim one inch further.

    An inch is a measure of distance, so use *farther*. I don't think I can swim one inch <u>farther</u>.

7. The doctor says that, judging by my shoe size, I should be about six foot tall when I finish growing.

    If you said that you are a six-foot guy, you'd be correct because the adjective *six-foot* comes before the noun *guy*. But in this case, this is correct: The doctor says that, judging by my shoe size, I should be about six <u>feet</u> tall when I finish growing.

8. The bag of chips fell down in back of the refrigerator.

    In back of is very informal. This is better: The bag of chips fell down <u>behind</u> the refrigerator.

Set # 17, page 165

1. Don't throw anything in the shark tank.

   No problem! I don't have any intention of jumping into the tank and throwing sharks around. Oh, wait—I bet you mean this: Don't throw anything <u>into</u> the shark tank.

2. I would of gotten you a present if I'd known it's your birthday.

   There's that sneaky word *of*. I would <u>have</u> gotten you a present if I'd known it's your birthday.

3. Did I do good on that last exercise?

   Yes, but you botched this one! It should be this: Did I do <u>well</u> [adverb describing the verb *do*] on that last exercise?

4. I was like no way when my brother tried to get me to eat some raw hamburger.

   This is a very clear sentence. However, it's also very informal and slangy. No good writer would write this way unless she is writing casual dialogue or deliberately trying to be funny. This is one way to make this sentence more formal without making it stuffy: I screamed, "Are you out of your itty bitty mind?!" when my brother tried to get me to eat some raw hamburger.

5. Have you got any cash on you?

   Very informal. To be more formal, try this: <u>Do you have</u> any cash on you?

6. I've been thinking lately how I'd like to learn to play a musical instrument.

   This is better: I've been thinking lately <u>that</u> I'd like to learn to play a musical instrument.

7. Sawyer and myself really appreciate your giving us a ride.

   There's that sneaky *myself*. Who needs it? Sawyer and I really appreciate your giving us a ride.

8. Good job! You skied very good today.

   The words *good* and *well* are mixed up very often in our language. The word *job* is a noun. Nouns always need adjectives (never adverbs) to describe them. *Good* is an adjective, so *good job* works fine. *Ski* is definitely an action verb, no doubt about that, and action verbs always need adverbs (never adjectives) to describe them. How did you ski? You skied very <u>well</u> today.

9. This is the end of this set of exercises. Its finished!

   Oh no—not *that* goof! This is the end of this set of exercises. <u>It's</u> finished!

Set # 18, page 175

1. The nervous hikers past a large, fresh pile of what looked suspiciously like bear scat.

   To pass is a verb; the word *past* is not a verb. The nervous hikers <u>passed</u> a large, fresh pile of what looked suspiciously like bear scat. If you write that the hikers *walked past* the pile, then the word *past* is correct; in this case it is used as a preposition.

2. Do you plan on updating your sports blog today?

   Plan on is very informal. This is better: Do you <u>plan</u> <u>to</u> update your sports blog today?

3. Sit your luggage down and come set for a few minutes.

   You could sit down on your luggage, but you cannot sit your luggage down. And if you set for a few minutes, there must be something in your hands that you are setting (placing) down. This is correct: <u>Set</u> your luggage down and come <u>sit</u> for a few minutes.

4. Did every one on the football team pass everyone of his final exams?

   Is *everyone* one word or two? This is correct: Did <u>everyone</u> on the team pass <u>every</u> [single] <u>one</u> of his final exams?

5. Joe is the chef whom cooked that fabulous stir fry.

   Does this sound right? Joe is the chef; him cooked that fabulous stir fry. No, it doesn't, so *whom* is not the word we want. Does this sound right? Joe is the chef; he cooked that fabulous stir fry. Yes, so *who* is the word we want. Joe is the chef <u>who</u> cooked that fabulous stir fry.

6. Jasmin is one of my friends which live in India.

   Use the word *which* with things and the word *who* for people. Jasmin is one of my friends <u>who</u> live in India.

7. My nose that has been stuffy all spring would appreciate a reduction in the pollen in the air.

   That has been stuffy all spring is a by-the-way phrase. Obviously you have only one nose (don't you?), so we know which nose you're talking about, and the sentence makes sense without this phrase. By-the-way phrases, which are not absolutely necessary, begin with *which*. My nose, <u>which</u> has been stuffy all spring, would appreciate a reduction in the pollen in the air.

8. Francine has lost more weight then Abigail.

   Then and *than* are often mixed up. Any time there is a comparison being made, *than* is the word you want. Francine has lost more weight <u>than</u> Abigail.

9. This is a long reign.

   I assume you mean the reign of Queen Elizabeth, in which case this sentence is fine.
   • If you're talking about weather: This is a long <u>rain</u>.
   • If you're talking about horsy stuff: This is a long <u>rein</u>.

10. What did you bring your racket for? It's snowing.

    What for is very informal. This is better: <u>Why</u> did you bring your racket? It's snowing.

11. I had this puppy when I was younger with a cute black patch on his left eye.

    The word *this* is a weakling unless you're referring to something right here, right now. You're talking about a puppy you had years ago, not one that's right here beside you right now. This is much better: I had <u>a</u> puppy when I was younger with a cute black patch on his left eye.

12. The grocery store which carries my favorite granola is the Trader Joe's on Main Street.

    Is the phrase *which carries my favorite granola* essential to this sentence or not? Let's try leaving it out: The grocery store is the

Trader Joe's on Main Street. That's not what you're trying to express. The part about your favorite granola is essential for this sentence to say what you intend to say. Essential phrases begin with *that*, not *which*. This is correct: The grocery store <u>that</u> carries my favorite granola is the Trader Joe's on Main Street.

13. Who did you give your outgrown tutu to?

Does this sound right: I gave my tutu to he? No, so *who* is not the word we want. Does this sound better: I gave my tutu to him? Yes, so *whom* is the word we want. <u>Whom</u> did you give your outgrown tutu to? This sentence ends with a preposition. Let's try to fix that. <u>To whom</u> did you give your outgrown tutu? That sounds okay for formal writing, but it sounds a little stuffy for everyday writing or conversation. We often choose our writing style based on whom and what we're writing for. (Yes, that sentence ends in a preposition, too.)

14. Its knot save two-holed you're breathe four two lounge.

What a bunch of mixed-up words! And just think—your spell-checker would not see a thing wrong with that sentence. I think you mean this: It's not safe to hold your breath for too long.

Chapter 5

Cleaning Up Messy Writing

The Fifteen Top Techniques for Correcting Messy Writing

We have talked a lot about grammar—parts of speech, how sentences are built, and making the various parts of our sentences agree with each other. We have talked a lot about punctuation and wacky words. All of these are very important parts of crisp, clean, creative writing. However, it's surprisingly easy to write a perfectly correct sentence with every punctuation mark in just the right place and every word spelled correctly and then realize that the sentence is goofy, boring, or even dumb. When I write, I try to let my words flow as quickly and effortlessly as I can, then I go back later—looking carefully at what I've written—and that's when I spot all the little messes that need to be cleaned up.

What are those messes that writers often make? Fortunately, there is a set of very common goofs, and if you learn how to spot them, you'll find it easy to clean up your words before anybody else reads them.

These fifteen clean-up pointers are not exactly rules. For example, you might decide that you really want to use a cliché in your writing, just as I've done here and there throughout this book, and that's fine. But if you know to watch for clichés, you'll pick just the right spot to use one and you'll sweep all the silly ones right off your pages.

Let's get started. Mess number one is one of my favorites: double talk.

Double talk
Repeating repeating yourself yourself

DOUBLE TALK:

The day was unforgettable. I will never forget it.

BETTER:

The day was unforgettable.

DOUBLE TALK:

I woke up about midnight because of a loud sound that woke me up.

BETTER:

I woke up about midnight because of a loud sound.

DOUBLE TALK:

I want apple pie à la mode with ice cream.

BETTER:

I want apple pie à la mode.

ALSO GOOD:

I want apple pie with ice cream.

How can you avoid double talk in your writing?

DOUBLE TALK:

It's simple: don't repeat the same thing <u>over and over</u> again.
(Over and over? Why not over and over and over and over and over?)

MORE DOUBLE TALK:

Don't repeat the same thing <u>over again</u>.
(*Over* and *again* mean the same thing.)

MORE DOUBLE TALK:

Don't <u>repeat</u> the same thing <u>again</u>.
(The word *repeat* means "to say something again.")

MORE DOUBLE TALK:

Don't <u>repeat the same thing</u>.
(What else are you going to repeat—a different thing? If so, you wouldn't be repeating.)

RIGHT AT LAST:

Don't repeat.

I know some of these sentences sound just fine, but that doesn't mean they *read* just fine. In conversation, we double-talk lots and lots (did you catch that one?).

Listening for double talk can be fun. Many expressions we use in everyday speech are redundant. Check these out:

first time ever	rarely ever	free gift
separate out	100% unanimous	small in size
9 PM in the evening	each and every one	red in color
return again	so forth and so on	square in shape
etc. etc.	one and the same	most unique
completely destroyed	past history	really truly
revert back	end result	new innovation
personal friend	local resident	sum total
usual customs	tuna fish	whole wide world
stalling for time	other alternative	few in number
mix together	rise up	the reason is because
rpms per minute	this point in time	
month of June	over and done with	the reason why
advance warning	continue on	in this day and time
true fact	untrue lie	
equally as important	extra additions	regular routine
may possibly	two polar opposites	final outcome
unexpected surprise	right beside	ATM machine

Excess baggage—unnecessary words
We often pad our sentences with words that are obvious and unnecessary.

When we speak, these words aren't earsores, but when we write, they are eyesores. They clutter our writing, making it unclear, rambling, and sloppy. When you proofread, be ruthless: slash words that don't need to be there.

WEAK:

I am sitting down on the chair.
(Where else would you sit—up?)

BETTER:

I am sitting on the chair.

WEAK:

I am diving down into the water.
(Do people ever dive sideways?)

BETTER:

I am diving into the water.

WEAK:

Will you please go and get my cell phone for me?

STILL WEAK:

Will you please go get my cell phone for me?

BETTER:

Will you please get my cell phone for me?

WRONG:

I needed a new book bag, and so my mom took me to buy one.
(*And* and *so* are both conjunctions—you need only one.)

RIGHT:

I needed a new book bag, and my mom took me to buy one.

Check out these unnecessary words:

I cleaned up all <u>of</u> my stuff.

This is some kind of <u>a</u> zebra, but I can't remember its name.

The doctor stitched <u>up</u> my cut.

I ate <u>a</u> half <u>of</u> my apple.

We're <u>all</u> out of toothpaste.

Put the dog outside <u>of</u> the house and bring the cat inside <u>of</u> the house.

I can't decide whether <u>or</u> <u>not</u> to go to the game.

I opened <u>up</u> my birthday gift before my birthday.

Eli admitted <u>to</u> hiding his sister's Barbie doll.

We have a tennis court reserved <u>up</u> until 6:00.

It would be better to eat a healthy meal before the soccer match <u>rather</u> than to load up on junk.

I don't have anything <u>that</u> special to wear to the prom.

It snowed all night <u>long</u>.

My parents haven't given me my birthday present <u>as</u> <u>of</u> yet.

When you finish ~~up~~ your work, you may go ~~out~~ to the party. By the way, where is the party ~~at~~?

REMINDER

Cut ~~out~~ those unnecessary words!

Blah blah blah—enough words to drown a fish
Good writing is crisp and clean.

"Garbage words" confuse your readers. Long sentences are not necessarily a sign of intelligence; in fact, they are often a sign of lazy writing. When you write, remember the KISS technique: Keep It Short and Simple.

Believe it or not, some professional writers are paid by the word; 20 cents a word is not uncommon, so *blah blah blah* could be worth 60 cents. Unfortunately, your language arts teacher will not hand you cash for padding your papers with a bunch of garbage words, so you might as well KISS.

BLAH BLAH BLAH:

At this point in time I really think that I need to start getting more of some kind of physical exercise.

CRISP:

I need to exercise more.

BLAH BLAH BLAH:

The reason why I left the door unlocked is because I was of the opinion that in the event that Dad got home during the time that I was out, he would be mad due to the fact that the door was locked.

CRISP:

I left the door unlocked because I thought Dad would be mad if he got home while I was out and found the door locked.

BLAH BLAH BLAH:

There are times in this day and age when I really feel very strongly that we should give more assistance to those who are currently homeless and have no place to live.

CRISP:

I feel strongly that we should assist the homeless more than we do.

Who needs all these words	when you can say this?
at that point in time	then
ahead of schedule	early
I am in possession of	I have
in advance of	before
it is my opinion that	I think
all of a sudden	suddenly
until such time as	until
in the event that	if
provided that	if
on the condition that	if
at a later date	later
due to the fact that	because
the reason why is that	because
owing to the fact that	because
had occasion to be	was
as a matter of fact	in fact
in spite of the fact that	although
there is no doubt but that	no doubt
first of all	first
during the time that	while

What about me?
Words that feel left out

I have encouraged you to delete words that you don't need. Now I'm going to encourage you not to leave out words you do need.

What would you think if your girlfriend or boyfriend said, "I like ice cream better than you"? You should definitely ask for clarification! Which does this mean:

- I like ice cream better than you like ice cream?
- I like ice cream better than I like you?

WRONG:

Mr. Jones, the physics teacher, called a meeting for students who hate physics and their parents.
(Anything else the students hate besides physics and their parents? Maybe squash or beets?)

RIGHT:

Mr. Jones, the physics teacher, called a meeting for students who hate physics and <u>for</u> their parents.

WRONG:

Is this movie similar or different from the last one you saw?

RIGHT:

Is this movie similar <u>to</u> or different from the last one you saw?

WRONG:

The mountains of Colorado are taller than Utah.

RIGHT:

The mountains of Colorado are taller than <u>those</u> <u>in</u> Utah.

WRONG:

I told you on Tuesday this would happen.

IS THIS WHAT YOU MEAN?

I told you <u>that</u> this would happen on Tuesday.

OR IS THIS WHAT YOU MEAN?

I told you on Tuesday <u>that</u> this would happen.

The weaklings—puny words
Don't water down your writing with trite words.

We overuse many words and phrases in everyday speech, and they've become hackneyed, banal, and vapid. *Vapid* —now there's a great word! It means "lacking taste, zest, or flavor; flat, stale, dull, or tedious"—all the ways you don't want your writing to sound. Search your writing for weaklings and substitute a juicy word, something with a little flair or pizzazz.

PUNY:

That's cool.

PIZZAZZ:

That's wonderful; that's fascinating; that's exciting.

MEGA-PUNY (WRITING DOESN'T GET MUCH WEAKER THAN THIS):

I wanted Craig to ask me to the prom so bad. It would've been real neat if he had, but, oh, well, he didn't. I went with Sam and we had a pretty nice time. You know, sometimes this sort of stuff turns out okay.

PIZZAZZ:

I wanted Craig to ask me to the prom. I waited eagerly for his call, but it never came. I went with Sam instead, and we had a great time together. Sometimes things work out well even when you expect that they won't.

(Don't worry—no one is asking you to talk this way, but written language is different from spoken language.)

Get tough with the weaklings—use some power-packed words:

Weak	Powerful
real pretty	beautiful
real cute	adorable
real mad	furious
real boring	monotonous
so much	extremely
so good	wonderful
so bad	terrible
so cool	really amazing
kind of nice	acceptable
not so great	disappointing
a whole lot	a great deal
pretty weak	frail
kind of bummed	depressed
lots of	countless

BRAIN TICKLERS   Set # 19

Find the goofs in these sentences and correct them.

1. Bring your rollerblades with you when you come to my house.

2. I rarely ever sleep late, but today I stayed in bed until noon.

3. Dad's new car is a blue Ford with a black interior, with power steering and power brakes, and with an engine with six cylinders.

4. There are some people who pad their sentences with unnecessary words.

5. Sometimes some people kind of feel like they should sort of try a little harder to like get more ahead of their game.

6. That movie is so cool; you'll just love it.

7. I like Lucy better than Frank.

8. I know you want to go ice skating. I also want to go ice skating, too.

9. It has seldom been the case that I have vacuumed my room without Mom's prodding me.

10. There are many reasons why you should eat plenty of vegetables.

11. I need to get me some vegetables to eat.

12. I have never and probably will never be a brave bungee jumper.

13. Fran is smarter than all the boys in the class.

14. The reason I did poorly on the test is because my dog ate my study sheets.

(Answers are on pages 206–207.)

Undernourished phrases
Vitamin therapy for your sentences

This is a sentence. It is grammatically correct and the punctuation is flawless. Do those facts make it a good sentence? Hardly. "This is a sentence" doesn't tell your reader anything very interesting. Check your writing for flat, dull, information-less sentences and give them a little nourishment. Don't add unnecessary filler words—add words power-packed with vitamins.

UNDERNOURISHED:

The kids quickly ate some food.

WITH SOME VITAMINS:

The boys quickly ate subs.

MORE VITAMINS:

The six boys quickly ate several foot-long subs.

MORE VITAMINS:

The six members of the boys' tennis team hungrily devoured several foot-long subs.

MORE VITAMINS:

The six members of the boys' tennis team hungrily devoured several foot-long subs after their tournament victory.

MEGA-VITAMINS:

Immediately after winning the regional tournament, the six members of the boys' tennis team hungrily devoured several foot-long subs, which Levi's mom had brought as a surprise.

UNDERNOURISHED:

A ball broke the neighbors' window.

WITH SOME VITAMINS:

A baseball accidentally broke the neighbors' window.

MORE VITAMINS:

A baseball, which Archer accidentally hit toward the neighbors' house, broke their window.

MORE VITAMINS:

A baseball, which Archer accidentally hit toward the neighbors' house, shattered their kitchen window.

MEGA-VITAMINS:

Archer's wild hit, which he accidentally slammed toward the neighbors' house, shattered their kitchen window.

Vague and foggy writing
What on earth are you talking about?

If you like to write on foggy days, go right ahead, but please edit your work before anyone else reads it. Unless you provide your readers with special fog-clearing goggles, nobody will understand what you're trying to say.

FOGGY:

These issues are sometimes related to other issues, and maybe there is a connection between all the things we've been talking about. You see, these are important questions that have been raised, and in the future somebody ought to answer them.

EXPLAIN YOURSELF:

These issues [what issues?] are sometimes [when?] related to [related in what ways?] other issues [what other issues?], and maybe [is there or isn't there?] there is a connection [what kind of connection?] between all the things [what things?] we've been talking about. You see [no, I certainly don't], these are important questions [what questions?] that have been raised [by whom?], and in the future [that's a very long time] somebody [who?] ought to [why ought they?] answer [how?] them.

FOGGY:

I am not really convinced that the jury's ideas were entirely fair. I think maybe he should have gotten off easier and maybe he didn't do it anyway because it's possible he was innocent.

CLEAR:

I am not convinced that the defendant was guilty in spite of the jury's verdict.

Double negatives
This is a no-no, so don't-don't!

WRONG:

You <u>don't</u> have <u>no</u> business using two negatives in the same clause. I <u>hardly never</u> make the double negative mistake, but when I do, my embarrassment is <u>unlike</u> <u>none</u> other.

RIGHT:

You <u>don't</u> have <u>any</u> business using two negatives in the same clause. I <u>hardly ever</u> make the double negative mistake, but when I do, my embarrassment is <u>like</u> <u>none</u> other.

WRONG:

I haven't seen no vampires around here lately.

RIGHT:

I haven't seen any vampires around here lately.

These are obvious negatives:

no, none, nobody, nowhere, nothing, no one, never, not, and words ending with *-n't* such as *can't, don't,* and *wouldn't*

These negatives are a little less obvious:
hardly, scarcely, barely, rarely, unlike

WRONG:

I don't see hardly any mess in my room.

RIGHT:

I see hardly any mess in my room.

ALSO RIGHT:

I don't see much mess in my room.

Check this out: double negatives actually cancel each other out!

> I didn't eat no pizza = I did eat some pizza.
> I hardly saw nothing = I did see something.
> I don't want no trouble from you = I do want some trouble from you.

Double negatives are used often in songs and in slang. Unless you're sure you want to break the rules, don't use them in formal writing.

SONG:

"I Can't Get No Satisfaction"

SLANG:

Ain't <u>no</u> way I'm eating that raw fish!
(Even though these cancel each other out and the literal meaning of this sentence is "There is a way I'm eating that raw fish," everybody knows its intended meaning.)

Notice that sometimes it is fine to have two negatives in a sentence. Just be sure that the negatives are not in the same clause.

RIGHT:

I <u>don't</u> want to keep going in circles feeling like I'm getting <u>nowhere</u>.
(*I don't want...*is a clause and *I'm getting nowhere* is another clause, so it is not wrong to have two negatives in this sentence.)

Run-ons—sentences that go on and on and on and on and on and on and on and on and on and on and on . . .
Run-on sentences are very hard for your reader to understand.

When one idea is complete, use a period. When a short group of thoughts or ideas is complete, end the paragraph and start a new one.

Sometimes when a sentence gets revved up, it's hard for the writer to know when to stop because many ideas are bubbling to the surface, and all the ideas seem related to each other and, therefore, appropriate to be included in the same sentence, and the sentence ends up going on and on . . . and on and on for what seems like forever so that, meanwhile, the poor, unsuspecting reader has almost no idea what's happening, can't remember what was happening at the beginning of the sentence, can't foresee where all this is leading, and wonders if maybe the writer's keyboard has a jammed period key and that's why there's never an end to the world's longest (and the universe's second most confusing) sentence, and it would be the universe's most confusing except for this, which actually is the longest and most confusing sentence in the annals of history: Once upon a time long ago in the land of ridiculously long sentences . . .

Help! Please stop!
This type of writing is guaranteed to
drive your readers crazy!

Goofy goofs—misplaced phrases
As you proofread, notice where you have placed descriptive phrases.

Phrases should usually be placed very close to the part of the sentence they describe. Careful proofreading can spare you some very embarrassing—and sometimes very funny—goofs.

GOOFY:
Three bicycles were reported stolen by the police yesterday.
(The phrase *by the police* comes right after the word *stolen*. It sounds as though you just can't trust those police!)

MUCH BETTER:
The police reported that three bicycles were stolen yesterday.

GOOFY:

Having cut his foot on the broken bottle, the doctor sewed Ted's wounds. (Did the doctor cut Ted's foot with a broken bottle? That's not very nice. Or did the doctor cut his own foot then sew up Ted? That's not very smart!)

MUCH BETTER:

The doctor sewed the wounds Ted received when he cut his foot on the broken bottle.

GOOFY:

After years of neglect in a basement closet, I found my old teddy bear and brought it to my room.
(I feel sorry for you. All those years in a basement closet must have been rough for you.)

MUCH BETTER:

I found my old teddy bear, which had been neglected for years in a basement closet, and brought it to my room.

GOOFY:

Ava ran to the teacher screaming her head off.
(I wonder what the teacher was so upset about.)

MUCH BETTER:

Ava, screaming her head off, ran to the teacher.

GOOFY:

Skiing on a cold, snowy day, icicles began to form on my eyelashes.
(Icicles on skis? I'd like to see that.)

MUCH BETTER:

Skiing on a cold, snowy day, I noticed icicles beginning to form on my eyelashes.

BRAIN TICKLERS   Set # 20

Find the goofs in these sentences and correct them.

1. The doctor said that if I don't start eating something other than Hershey bars within a month my brain will be solid chocolate.

2. That movie is unlike none other I've seen.

3. I went to visit my cousin in Atlanta because my parents were going on a trip to California, a trip they had looked forward to for a long time, and my cousin and I, along with several of her friends, had a great time shopping, seeing movies, and doing other things, like water skiing and snorkeling, that I had wanted to do for a long time but hadn't had a chance to do because my parents said it was more important for me to focus on school work, especially on improving my writing skills.

4. Finley led his pet alligator, holding his head high with pride, into the winner's circle at the pet show.

5. Isabela watched the lion approach wide-eyed with fear.

6. Johnny is so sleepy he doesn't hardly remember his own name.

7. I told my mom I wanted to go to the mall to buy some supplies for my science project, and that is what happened.

8. Hannah served dessert to her friends on paper plates.

9. I think that maybe we should do something to improve the conditions of some people who are in some sort of trouble.

(Answers are on pages 208–209.)

Keeping everything consistent—parallel construction
Have you heard the old saying about changing horses in midstream?

Picture it in your mind—crossing a rapidly flowing stream on horseback and changing horses halfway across. Not a good idea. You're wondering what this has to do with writing a language arts paper? I'll show you. This is how it looks when you change horses in mid-sentence:

INCONSISTENT:

I like playing baseball, reading about sports, and tacos.
> playing baseball = gerund phrase
> reading about sports = gerund phrase
> tacos = noun

CONSISTENT:

I like playing baseball, reading about sports, and eating tacos.
> playing baseball = gerund phrase
> reading about sports = gerund phrase
> eating tacos = gerund phrase

INCONSISTENT:

We're studying equations, all about Europe, and to write well.

equations = noun
all about Europe = prepositional phrase
to write well = infinitive phrase

CONSISTENT:

We're studying equations, European history, and writing techniques.

equations = noun
history = noun
techniques = noun

INCONSISTENT:

Annabelle swung the bat and the ball was hit.

Annabelle swung = active voice
the ball was hit = passive voice

CONSISTENT:

Annabelle swung the bat and hit the ball.

Annabelle swung = active voice
(Annabelle) hit = active voice

Keeping it consistent also applies to the format of your writing. Notice how this section has been formatted.

- INCONSISTENT always comes before CONSISTENT.
- INCONSISTENT and CONSISTENT are always in capital letters.
- There is a colon after each INCONSISTENT and each CONSISTENT.
- The indentations are all the same.

I could have formatted this page many different ways, but once I picked a style, I stuck with it. That's consistency—and it makes for easier reading. How might this page have looked if I had not been consistent? Here is the same example written two different ways—you decide which is easier to read.

inconsistent: James says yes, Meg says no, and Emily said maybe. This is INCONSISTENT because it mixes verb tenses. Consistent: James says yes, Meg says no, and Emily says maybe. Of course, it would also be consistent and correct to write it this way: James says, "Yes," Meg says, "No," and Emily says, "Maybe."

INCONSISTENT:

James says yes, Meg says no, and Emily said maybe.
(This is inconsistent because it mixes verb tenses.)

CONSISTENT:

James says yes, Meg says no, and Emily says maybe.

ALSO CORRECT:

James says, "Yes," Meg says, "No," and Emily says, "Maybe."

Get smart—powering up your brain cells
When editing sentences, a writer must also edit his/her logic.

Get tough and ask yourself, does this make good sense? Does it make *any* sense?

I DON'T THINK SO:

I want to see what you have to say.
(Do you know many people who hear with their eyes?)

NOW YOU'RE THINKING:

I want to hear what you have to say.

I DON'T THINK SO:

The hundred-year-old man rode his hundred-year-old horse down the hundred-year-old road to his cabin.
(Check with a vet—how many horses live to the age of 100?)

NOW YOU'RE THINKING:

The hundred-year-old man rode his feeble, old horse down the hundred-year-old road to his cabin.

I DON'T THINK SO:

The pirates sailed all seven continents seeking treasure.
(They must have had awesome ships if they could sail on land!)

NOW YOU'RE THINKING:

The pirates sailed all five oceans seeking treasure.

I DON'T THINK SO:

In our city, 80 percent of the children go to public school, 30 percent go to private school, and 3 percent are home schooled.
(Let's see, 80 percent + 30 percent + 3 percent = 113 percent. That's a lot of kids!)

NOW YOU'RE THINKING:

In our city, 80 percent of the children go to public school, 18 percent go to private school, and 2 percent are home schooled.

Chop chop chop
Tasteless bites vs. delicious sentences

Choppy sentences and paragraphs are dull and boring. Don't make sentences so short they sound like a two-year-old learning to talk. And don't use one-sentence paragraphs except for very strong emphasis. If you have only one sentence, weave that sentence into another paragraph.

BORING:

My cat's name is Boris. My dog's name is Bowser. My hamster's name is Sunny. My boa constrictor's name is Tough Stuff. I have four pets. Those are my pets.

BETTER:

I have four pets: a cat named Boris, a dog named Bowser, a hamster named Sunny, and a boa constrictor named Tough Stuff.

EVEN BETTER:

I have four great pets! Boris the cat gets along well with Bowser the dog, but Sunny the hamster stays as far away as possible from Tough Stuff the boa constrictor.

BORING:

I wanted to go to the store. My mom took me to the store. I saw a new video game there. I wanted the game. My mom let me buy it. I was happy. This paragraph is about as exciting as soggy cereal.

BETTER:

I wanted to go to the store, so my mom took me. I saw a new video game there that I wanted, and my mom let me buy it. I was happy, and this paragraph is a little better. But not much.

EVEN BETTER:

I heard about a great new video game from a friend, and I was excited to see it for myself. My mom was busy, but I sweet-talked her into taking me to the store. When I actually played the game on the store's demo system, it was far better than I had expected, and, believe it or not, my mom agreed to get it for me. I was ecstatic and, best of all, on the drive home Mom taught me how to write paragraphs that don't remind my readers of soggy cereal.

What makes this last example strong? It contains an interesting mixture of sentence types: short and long, simple and more complex.

☝ PAINLESS TIP

If your writing sounds dull to you, spice it up with interesting words, varied sentence lengths, different styles of sentences, and points of emphasis.

(See pages 65–66 for more on different types of sentences.)

Repetition repetition repetition
Think up a new, zesty word.

REPETITIVE:

The football game was great. Our football team played great even though a storm came in during the game. It was very stormy and the guys got wet. Even though they were wet, they played great. They went to the locker room all wet and muddy, but they were happy. Everybody was happy! Well, everyone was happy except our rival team, who were also wet but unhappy.

If a dictionary is the writer's best friend, a thesaurus is his or her second-best friend. The English language is too full of interesting words to keep using the same ones. For example, the online thesaurus I checked gives 116 synonyms for the word *great*.

Great = supreme, wonderful, sensational, magnificent, superb, tops, unexcelled, winning, world-class, A-1, impressive, phenomenal, exceptional

Wet = soaked, drenched, dripping, moist, saturated, sodden, water-logged, watery

Storm = cloudburst, downpour, precipitation, squall, blast, inclement weather

Happy = thrilled, joyful, ecstatic, delighted, elated, flying high, gleeful, jubilant, pleased

MUCH BETTER:

The football game was spectacular. Our team played superbly even though there was a downpour during the third quarter. Although the guys were drenched, they played an outstanding game. They went to the locker room soggy and muddy, but they were ecstatic. Everybody was flying high! Well, everyone except our rival team, who were water-logged and woebegone.

Sometimes repetition works. If the writer uses it skillfully, repetition creates emphasis.

We have nothing to fear but fear itself.
Beauty is as beauty does.
. . . of the people, by the people, for the people

More often, repetition makes a sentence sound weak or wacky.

WACKY:

One thing that I would like to do would be to maybe be a pilot.

BETTER:

I might like to be a pilot.

WACKY:

Julianne told me that she thought that what that noise was was thunder that was so loud that it was deafening, and I think that she was right—that that was what it was.

BETTER:

Julianne told me she thought the noise was deafeningly loud thunder. I think she was right.

WACKY:

I spoke to my dad on the phone, and when I told him where I was, I was mad that he was mad that I was where I was.

BETTER:

I spoke to my dad on the phone. When I told him where I was, he was angry—and that made *me* angry!

Clichés
Not that same old phrase again

Blind as a bat, cool as a cucumber, and *happy as a clam*—they are all clichés. A cliché is an overused expression. A million writers have used the expression before you, and a million will use it after you. So why use it? With so many spicy words in the English language, usually you can come up with something more clever than the same-old same-old.

Count the clichés in this story:

Last night I was hungry as a bear. I told my mom I wanted a really big dinner because I knew I could eat like a pig. She said, "Let's go to McDonald's."

We left the house in a flash. As soon as we got to McDonald's, I could tell that something fishy was going on. There was not a soul to be seen. It was as plain as the nose on my face that they were closed for the duration, so we headed out for Bob's Grill.

Bob's Grill was neither closed nor crowded—in fact, there was room to spare. By that time I was hungry to beat the band, and I ordered enough barbecued ribs to choke a horse. When they came, I was up to my ears in ribs, but, believe it or not, I ate every last one.

Later in the evening I was sick as a dog. That just goes to show you: sometimes your eyes are bigger than your stomach. My mom gave me some Pepto Bismol, which I drank like water, and then I slept like a baby.

The moral of this story is this: go nice and easy when you order ribs at Bob's.

How many clichés did you count? Did you catch all of these?

hungry as a bear	eat like a pig
in a flash	not a soul to be seen
something fishy going on	for the duration
as plain as the nose	room to spare
on my face	enough to choke a horse
headed out	believe it or not
to beat the band	sick as a dog
up to my ears	your eyes are bigger than
every last one	your stomach
just goes to show you	slept like a baby
drank like water	nice and easy
the moral of the story	

CAUTION—Major Mistake Territory!

Clichés aren't wrong; they're just worn out. Use them occasionally or for a special effect, but don't use many or your writing will be as soggy as a dishcloth (catch that one?).

Here are some more clichés:

crazy as a loon	rock the boat
easy as pie	muddy the water
high as a kite	have time to kill
skinny as a rail	down and out
smart as a whip	ripe old age
mad as a hornet	there's more in store
naked as a jay bird	raining cats and dogs
loose as a goose	down in the dumps
bright as a button	cry over spilled milk
hard as nails	heart-to-heart talk
strong as an ox	on the tip of your tongue
fresh as a daisy	take a rain check
thick as thieves	for crying out loud
tight as a drum	eat your heart out

BRAIN TICKLERS   Set # 21

Find the goofs in these sentences and correct them.

1. I bought a great new coat for cold winter days. Tuesday was colder than the weatherman had said it would be, and I hadn't worn my coat. I was so cold I thought I'd die of cold!

2. Peter was at Debbie's house. He heard a strange sound. He went into the living room. He was surprised to hear the parrot calling "out." Peter let the bird out. The parrot's name is Loud Mouth.

3. I needed a new blouse. Red is my favorite color. I bought a new blouse. It's red. I like it.

4. My friend Emily, my cousin Brinley, and Laney (my sister) asked me if I wanted fried chicken, something gooey like fudge cake, or to eat something healthier like a salad.

5. Half the kids ordered hamburgers, half ordered chicken, and a few ordered enchiladas.

6. If I've said it once, I've said it a thousand times: Don't use a whole heaping bunch of unnecessary, extra words; don't write a slew of over-the-top and melodramatic words in your paper; don't use a mess of

wishy-washy, blah-de-blah words; and don't use redundant, repetitive, over and over again words lots and lots of times if you don't want your writing to look reeeellly bad.

7. I'm dead tired, flat broke, and I'm having a bad hair day to boot.

(Answers are on pages 209–211.)

BRAIN TICKLERS—THE ANSWERS
Set # 19, page 191

1. Bring your rollerblades with you when you come to my house.

    There's nothing wrong with this sentence, but you can make it crisper by leaving out two words: Bring your rollerblades when you come to my house.

2. I rarely ever sleep late, but today I stayed in bed until noon.

    Rarely ever is a commonly used phrase, but it's double talk. I rarely sleep late, but today I stayed in bed until noon.

3. Dad's new car is a blue Ford with a black interior, with power steering and power brakes, and with an engine with six cylinders.

    Who needs all those *with*'s? Dad's new car is a blue Ford with a black interior, power steering, power brakes, and a six-cylinder engine.

4. There are some people who pad their sentences with unnecessary words.

    There's nothing wrong with this sentence, but this is much crisper: Some people pad their sentences with unnecessary words.

5. Sometimes some people kind of feel like they should sort of try a little harder to like get more ahead of their game.

    This is foggy and full of puny words. Here is one way to clean it up: Some students in my class wisely believe it's a good idea to work a little harder and study a little more in order to be "at the top of their game."

6. That movie is so cool; you'll just love it.

    Fine for conversation, puny for a language arts paper. That movie is outstanding; you'll love it.

7. I like Lucy better than Frank.

    Some words are missing. Which of these do you mean?
    *   I like Lucy better than Frank likes Lucy.
    *   I like Lucy better than I like Frank.

8. I know you want to go ice skating. I also want to go ice skating, too.

    The second sentence contains double talk. *Also* and *too* mean exactly the same thing. Both of these are correct:
    *   I want to go ice skating, too.
    *   I also want to go ice skating.

9. It has seldom been the case that I have vacuumed my room without Mom's prodding me.

    Too wordy. Seldom have I vacuumed my room without Mom's prodding me.

10. There are many reasons why you should eat plenty of vegetables.

    The reason why is double talk. Knock out *why* and the sentence will be fine. There are many reasons you should eat plenty of vegetables.

11. I need to get me some vegetables to eat.

    What's that *me* doing there? Both of these are correct:
    *   I need to get some vegetables to eat.
    *   I need to get myself some vegetables to eat.

12. I have never and probably will never be a brave bungee jumper.

    A necessary word has been left out. I have never <u>been</u> and probably will never be a brave bungee jumper.

13. Fran is smarter than all the boys in the class.

    A word might be missing. If Fran is a girl, this sentence is perfect. If Fran is a boy, it should be this: Fran is smarter than all the *other* boys in the class.

14. The reason I did poorly on the test is because my dog ate my study sheets.

    The reason is because is double talk. Both of these are correct:
    *   The reason I did poorly on the test is that my dog ate my study sheets.
    *   I did poorly on the test because my dog ate my study sheets.

Set # 20, pages 196–197

1. The doctor said that if I don't start eating something other than Hershey bars within a month my brain will be solid chocolate.

    The phrase *within a month* is confusing. Do you need to start eating better within a month, or will your brain be chocolate within a month? Both of these are correct:
    *   The doctor said that if I don't start eating something other than Hershey bars within a month, my brain will be solid chocolate. (Notice that the comma makes it clear.)
    *   The doctor said that if I don't start eating something other than Hershey bars, my brain will be solid chocolate within a month.

2. That movie is unlike none other I've seen.

    Unlike none is a double negative. These are both correct:
    *   That movie is like none other I've seen.
    *   That movie is unlike any other I've seen.

3. I went to visit my cousin in Atlanta because my parents were going on a trip to California, a trip they had looked forward to for a long time, and my cousin and I, along with several of her friends, had a great time shopping, seeing movies, and doing other things, like water skiing and snorkeling, that I had wanted to do for a long time but hadn't had a chance to do because my parents said it was more important for me to focus on school work, especially on improving my writing skills.

    Whew! If that run-on sentence ran on much longer, it could fill an entire book. Try breaking it into three or four separate sentences.

4. Finley led his pet alligator, holding his head high with pride, into the winner's circle at the pet show.

    Who is holding his head high—Finley or the alligator? Putting the description closer to the name Finley clears up the confusion. Finley, holding his head high with pride, led his pet alligator into the winner's circle at the pet show.

5. Isabela watched the lion approach wide-eyed with fear.

It sounds as though the lion is scared of Isabela! Wide-eyed with fear, Isabela watched the lion approach.

6. Johnny is so sleepy he doesn't hardly remember his own name.

   The problem is a double negative: *not hardly*. Johnny is so sleepy he hardly remembers his own name.

7. I told my mom I wanted to go to the mall to buy some supplies for my science project, and that is what happened.

   And that is what happened is very vague. What happened? You told your mom or you went to the mall? I told my mom I wanted to go to the mall to buy some supplies for my science project, so she took me.

8. Hannah served dessert to her friends on paper plates.

   Her friends were on paper plates? I'd like to see that! Hannah served dessert on paper plates to her friends.

9. I think that maybe we should do something to improve the conditions of some people who are in some sort of trouble.

   Thick fog! We who? Do what? For what people? What conditions and what sort of trouble? Be specific and be clear. This is one possibility: I firmly believe that our government should do more to improve the living conditions of migrant farm workers.

Set # 21, pages 204–205

1. I bought a great new coat for cold winter days. Tuesday was colder than the weatherman had said it would be, and I hadn't worn my coat. I was so cold I thought I'd die of cold!

   The word *cold* is used four times. Try this: I bought a great new coat for winter days. Tuesday was colder than the weatherman had said it would be, and I hadn't worn my coat. I thought I'd freeze!

2. Peter was at Debbie's house. He heard a strange sound. He went into the living room. He was surprised to hear the parrot calling "out." Peter let the bird out. The parrot's name is Loud Mouth.

   This paragraph is very choppy. There are many possible ways to improve it. Here is one way: While he was at Debbie's house,

Peter heard a strange sound coming from the living room. When he realized that the sound was Loud Mouth, Debbie's parrot, calling "out," Peter let the bird out of the cage.

3. I needed a new blouse. Red is my favorite color. I bought a new blouse. It's red. I like it.

    This is very choppy. Try something juicier. Red is my favorite color, so when I needed a new blouse, I chose a beautiful one in a soft shade of rose.

4. My friend Emily, my cousin Brinley, and Laney (my sister) asked me if I wanted fried chicken, something gooey like fudge cake, or to eat something healthier like a salad.

    There are two cases of inconsistency in this sentence. My friend Emily, my cousin Brinley, and my sister Laney asked me if I wanted fried chicken, something gooey like fudge cake, or something healthier like a salad.

5. Half the kids ordered hamburgers, half ordered chicken, and a few ordered enchiladas.

    Wake up, brain cells, wake up! How many kids does this make?

6. If I've said it once, I've said it a thousand times: Don't use a whole heaping bunch of unnecessary, extra words; don't write a slew of over-the-top and melodramatic words in your paper; don't use a mess of wishy-washy, blah-de-blah words; and don't use redundant, repetitive, over and over again words lots and lots of times if you don't want your writing to look *reeeellly* bad.

    If I've said it once, I've said it a thousand times is a cliché. *A whole heaping bunch of unnecessary and extra words* contains a whole heaping bunch of unnecessary words. *A slew of over-the-top and melodramatic words* is quite melodramatic. *Wishy-washy* and *blah-de-blah* are wishy-washy words. *Redundant, repetitive, over and over again,* and *lots and lots* contains more double talk (redundant words) than I can count. And *reeeellly* bad looks far worse than really bad. Every mark of punctuation in this sentence is perfect, yet this sentence is so horrible that there's no hope for it. Let's just pronounce it unfixable.

7. I'm dead tired, flat broke, and I'm having a bad hair day to boot.

   One sentence, four clichés: *dead tired, flat broke, bad hair day*, and *to boot*. Since this is the last exercise of the chapter, let's let sleeping dogs lie (another cliché) and call it quits (another cliché). Whatta ya have to say about that (another cliché)?

Chapter 6

Writing a Good E-mail

Not so many years ago, e-mail was brand new. When it first came out, many teachers and writers were concerned that the informal way people write e-mails would have a bad effect on people's writing in general. However, before e-mail, people rarely wrote letters and almost always used the phone to communicate with each other. Now we're writing again, and that's great.

Some Guidelines

Just as there are some rules and guidelines for writing a good paper, there are some guidelines for writing a good e-mail. As with all other types of good writing, how you write depends on to whom you're writing. Keeping your audience in mind is supremely important when you are composing an e-mail. An e-mail to your grandmother would be different from an e-mail to your sister, and that would be different from an e-mail to an Internet business that you'd like some information from. For example, check these out:

GOOD E-MAIL TO A FRIEND:

Dude, can you believe I totally lost that web address you gave me? Shoot it back at me.

GOOD E-MAIL TO YOUR GRANDMOTHER:

Hi Grandma. You know that website you said I'd love? Bummer—I lost it! I thought I surely put that piece of paper in my pocket, but I've looked everywhere and can't find it. Will you send it to me again? Thanks—and here comes a big virtual hug for my favorite person.

GOOD E-MAIL TO YOUR TEACHER:

Hi Mrs. Smythe. You know that website you recommended I check out? I was sure I had that piece of paper in my pocket, but now I can't find it. Would you please e-mail it to me? Thanks so much, and I'm sorry for the extra trouble. See you tomorrow.

GOOD E-MAIL TO YOUR BOSS:

Mr. Stein, you told me about a website that you recommended I check out. Unfortunately, I have lost the piece of paper I wrote that web address on. Could you please e-mail me the address? I'll check it out right away. Thank you very much.

Make your reader's job easy

Most people find reading on a computer monitor or cell phone harder on their eyes than reading on paper.

Here are some things to remember to make reading your e-mail a pleasure instead of hard work:

- Keep sentences relatively short.
- Keep paragraphs relatively short.
- Double space between paragraphs.
- Use a clean, simple, easy-to-read font.

HARD TO READ ON SCREEN:

Hi there, Brinley. How have you been doing since summer camp? Remember that book I told you about? Did you read it yet and did you like it because I found another one by the same author that I thought you'd like, so let me know if you liked the first one and I'll send you the name of the new one. I'd love to see you again soon. Are you going back to camp this summer? Let's see if we can bunk together!

EASY TO READ ON SCREEN:

Hi there, Brinley. How have you been doing since summer camp?

Remember that book I told you about? Did you read it yet? Did you like it? I found another one by the same author I thought you'd like. Let me know if you liked the first one and I'll send you the name of the new one.

I'd love to see you again soon. Are you going back to camp this summer? Let's see if we can bunk together!

Say hello nicely
The style for salutations in e-mail is different from the style in letters.

In letters we almost always start out with "Dear Sally" for a friendly letter and "Dear Sirs" for a more formal letter. People are not using that style with e-mails very often, partly because e-mail is less formal than handwritten or printed letters. Here are some other commonly used and very polite salutations:

> Good morning, Mr. Smith, (formal)
> Mr. Smith,
> Susie, (informal, to a friend)
> Hi, Grandma
> Happy Birthday, Grandpa!
> Hello, Ms. Lancaster

Punctuate with precision
Sometimes less is more.

Many people overuse exclamation marks, ellipses, and dashes in e-mails. They are all fine in moderation, but don't overlook the plain little period. It deserves a spot in e-mails, too!

TOO MUCH:

Hey Aunt Samantha . . . thanks way much (!!) for that fabulous sweater for my birthday . . . I love it!!! The color is just absolutely perfect (!) with my new skirt —— also with my favorite blouse —— and it doesn't look half shabby with the way cool jeans Dad got me for my birthday . . . we had a great time that day . . . wish you coulda been here! Lotsa love . . . Kate

JUST RIGHT:

Hey, Aunt Samantha. Thanks way much for that fabulous sweater for my birthday. I love it! The color is just absolutely perfect with my new skirt—also with my favorite blouse. And it doesn't look half shabby with the way cool jeans Dad got me for my birthday. We had a great time that day. Wish you coulda been here! Lotsa love, Kate.

Write it right
Use proper spelling, grammar, and punctuation in your e-mails.

Because it's "just an e-mail" and because it's a fast form of communication doesn't mean there's no need to proofread and edit your words. Sloppiness in an e-mail makes your message hard to read and, worse, hard to take seriously. And remember that messages posted on a forum, on a blog, or on social media may live there for a very long time. You want your words to look good on the web!

SLOPPY:

Hay there, Liz, whazzup! I'm going to get to practise kinda late cuz, I gotta take my sister to the babysister—cool . . . do don't be worry . . . I'll get there whenever I gt there . . .!

CASUAL BUT CLEAN:

Hey there, Liz. What's up? I'm going to get to practice kind of late because I have to take my sister to the babysitter. So don't be worried—I'll get there whenever I get there.

Be careful with emphasis
Don't SCREAM at your reader!

DO NOT WRITE YOUR WHOLE E-MAIL IN CAPITALS. IT FEELS TO YOUR READERS LIKE YOU'RE SHOUTING AT THEM, and they probably won't like it. If you want to emphasize a word or phrase, it's fine to use caps or underlining, but don't do it often.

Be clear in the subject line
A clear subject line is like a clear title to a paper.

You wouldn't title your term paper "Stuff about Interesting Stuff." A clear subject tells your e-mail reader what to expect, and it is especially important if you're writing to someone you don't know well or if you have an unusual e-mail address.

I'M NOT SURE I'D OPEN THIS ONE:

FROM: sharkdog@aol.com
SUBJECT: you got the info?

THIS ONE I'D OPEN:

FROM: sharkdog@aol.com
SUBJECT: a question from Sue Brown about our field trip

I'M NOT SURE I'D OPEN THIS ONE:

FROM: xjv45l@hotmail.com
SUBJECT: ya good

THIS ONE I'D OPEN:

FROM: xjv45l@hotmail.com
SUBJECT: I loved your performance in the school play

Be polite and clear in your message
Don't be so terse that you sound rude.

E-mail is a fast way to communicate. Type it, send it, and the other person receives it almost instantly. Sometimes when we write fast, we leave out too many words and the person receiving the message may find it to be a mishmash of confusing words and bad manners. Keep it short and sweet, but make sure your reader will not only really understand what you're saying, but also know just how to interpret what you're feeling.

UNCLEAR:

Could U plz send info on your state.

CLEAR:

My class is studying the history of Virginia. My project is on the historic battlefields in the Shenandoah Valley. Could you please send me some information or refer me to good websites? Thank you very much.

UNCLEAR AND NOT VERY SWEET:

Hi Grandma. We're still on. See ya.

CLEAR AND SWEET:

Hi Grandma. We're still on for lunch on Saturday. We'll be at your house at noon. Can't wait to see ya!

SOUNDS RUDE:

Tomorrow at 10.

MUCH BETTER:

Thanks for your quick reply. Tomorrow at 10 is great. See you then.

Don't go overboard with abbrev.
Sometimes writing it out the long way is best.

Why do people love to abbreviate in e-mails and text messages? It saves keystrokes and often looks cute. But it can also get confusing, and not everybody understands those funky abbreviations.

NOW THAT'S CONFUSING:

BTW, FWIW I was ROTFL when I got your last e-mail. QT! TTFN.

WHEW, THANKS:

By the way, for what it's worth, I was rolling on the floor laughing when I got your last e-mail. Cute! Ta ta for now.

Here are a few of the abbreviations often seen in texts and e-mails:

Abbreviation	Meaning
BTW	by the way
IMHO	in my humble opinion
FWIW	for what it's worth
LOL	laugh out loud
ROTFL	rolling on the floor laughing
TTFN	ta ta for now
TTYL	talk to you later
FYI	for your information
BCNU	be seeing you

Don't make too many faces!
As with abbreviations, sometimes it's better to write it out the long way.

Why do people love smiley faces in e-mails and texts? It's important to remember that these ways of communicating lack the "body language" of face-to-face conversations. You can tell by your mother's body language, facial expression, and tone of voice whether "I need to talk to you" is good news or bad news. People can't tell those things in e-mails, so they compensate by using smileys to express emotions.

CASUAL AND A BIT SILLY:

I'm so :) with my new puppy. I'd be mighty : (if he chews Mom's new sofa. I think I'll suggest to him that he not   ;)

MUCH BETTER:

I'm so happy with my new puppy :) I sure hope he doesn't chew on Mom's new sofa. I think I'll suggest to him that he not.

⚡ CAUTION—Major Mistake Territory!

Smileys are called emoticons—emotion icons. Using a few in an e-mail or a text to a friend is not a problem. Using them in professional e-mails or using them when you're trying to create a good first impression is usually not a great idea. Not everyone understands them or likes them.

Spelling checks
Remember to check your spelling before you hit "send."

In the English language, spelling is a bear. Why do we put a final *e* on the word *were* and then pronounce it as though it had a *u* in the middle and no *e* at all? Doesn't it seem phunny to you that *pneumonia* begins with a *p* and that *phone* does not begin with an *f*?

We're mighty lucky to live in the age of computer spelling checkers, but even when you use your spelling checker on your word processing application or on your e-mail program, you still must proofread carefully. Computers don't know the difference between *write, rite,* and *right.* They are all spelled correctly.

In a sentences that look lack thus, you're computer wood nut sea any thin wrung because all these warts is spilled write.

The Old-Fashioned Way
When not to write e-mails

As wonderful as e-mail is, it is still less formal than a printed letter and less personal than a handwritten letter. Writing a polite or sweet e-mail to someone is never a bad thing to do, but every now and then, a letter is better. It's as if there's a little more of you in a

handwritten letter than in an e-mail, no matter how well written the
e-mail may be.

NOT A GREAT E-MAIL:

Grandpa, that was a good birthday present. Thanks.

IMAGINE THIS AS A HANDWRITTEN LETTER:

Dear Grandpa,

What a wonderful birthday present! I'd been wanting a digital camera of my
own for a while. I can't wait to use it. I'll e-mail you some of my best pictures.
Thanks again, and I can't wait to see you at Thanksgiving.

Chapter 7

Getting It All Together

Editing a Paper

What is the difference between the way students write and the way professionals write?

Easy question—here is the difference:

Average student: write it, hand it in

Above-average student: write it, edit it, rewrite it, hand it in

Exceptional student: write it, edit it, rewrite it, edit it, rewrite it, hand it in

Professional writer: write it, edit it, rewrite it, edit it, rewrite it, edit it, rewrite it, hand it in

Let's see what that looks like.

Think, write, edit

Now we're going to pull together everything we have learned in this book.

The assignment for social studies class is to write a short paper titled "Should Man Explore Space or Stay at Home?" Here is my first draft. It's a mess. Help me clean it up.

Some people say its a real dumb idea for man to explore outer space, they say its like stupid to spend all that money on astronauts when people here at home need the money. I am of the opinion that this is wrong. We should get to know more about our universe. And after all good stuff has already come from the space porgram. NASA has invented all kinds of cool stuff. I believe man should continue to explore space and other places that might make life better here on this plant. If I was president, I'd make sure that happens.

Step 1: Check spelling.

There are four spelling errors in this piece. Did you catch them? We need to change *porgram* to *program*, and we need to change *plant* to *planet*. And that sneaky *its* crept in twice! Both times it should be *it is*, or *it's*.

Step 2: Check for punctuation mistakes.

The first sentence and the second sentence are linked by a comma, and a comma is too weak for that job. A semicolon would be okay, but making them two separate sentences is probably better.

And after all good stuff needs a comma after the word *all*. Without it, the reader stumbles a bit.

Step 3: Check for verb mistakes.

Two verb mistakes are in the last sentence. *If I was president* is a "what if" statement, so it needs the subjunctive; it should be *if I were president*. The last half of that sentence has an awkward mix of verb tenses. It would sound better this way: *I'd make sure that happened.*

Step 4: Check for adverb and adjective mistakes.

Real dumb is dumb! *Dumb* is an adjective, so it needs an adverb to modify it. *Really dumb* is correct.

Step 5: Check for unnecessary words.

To say *I am of the opinion that* is not wrong, but it's wordy. Instead, use *I believe*.

Step 6: Check for colloquialisms, slang, and informal phrases.

They say it's like stupid is very slangy. Let's drop the word *like*.

Step 7: Check for dumb or illogical statements.

Don't fret over dumb statements—we all make them in our first drafts! *They say it's stupid to spend all that money on astronauts.* Actually, all the money is not being spent on astronauts. It's being spent on the space program in general.

I believe man should continue to explore space and other places that might make life better here on this planet. Do you see what's illogical here? If we've included all of space (in other words, the entire universe) in the first part of the sentence, what other places are there to explore?

Step 8: Check paragraphing.

This is all one paragraph. Does it read well that way? No, so let's change that.

After the first round of cleanup, this is what we have:

Some people say it's a really dumb idea for man to explore outer space. They say it's stupid to spend all that money on the space program when people here at home need the money.

I believe this is wrong. We should get to know more about our universe. And after all, good stuff has already come from the space program. NASA has invented all kinds of cool stuff.

I believe man should continue to explore space in an effort to make life better here on this planet. If I were president, I'd make sure that happened.

It's better, but it's still weak. Let's keep working on it.

Step 9: Look for vague phrases.

I believe this is wrong contains that vague word *this.* How about *I believe their objections are wrong.*

All that money is vague. How much money? We could google the annual budget for NASA, or we could write *billions of dollars for each mission.*

Step 10: Look for repetition of words or phrases.

Stuff is always a vague word, and it's very informal as well. *Cool stuff* is even more slangy than just plain stuff. We've used the word *stuff* twice in the second paragraph and both should disappear.

Step 11: Look for weak sentences and phrases that need some more information.

Some people say . . . What people? How many people? Do a little research on the Internet and you might find a very helpful statistic. *A recent survey indicates that 28% of the American population believes* . . .

The word *dumb* is weak. Let's go for something strong, like *foolish. Stupid* is also a weak word. Let's change that to *irresponsible*.

People here at home need the money is a bit weak. Let's provide more information and say that people here at home pre in need of improvements in housing, education, and health care.

And after all, good technology has already come . . . *NASA has invented all kinds of cool stuff* . . . What good technology? What cool stuff? This is really the heart of this paper, but there are not any examples to back up this position. All it took was a visit to the NASA website to find the power-packed examples that make a huge difference in this paper.

After the second round of cleanup, this is what we have:

A recent survey indicates that 28% of the American population believes that it's a really foolish idea for man to explore outer space. They say it's irresponsible to spend billions of dollars for each mission of the space program when people here at home are in need of improvements in housing, education, and health care.

I believe their objections are wrong. We should get to know more about our universe. And after all, good technology has already come from the space program. NASA has invented all kinds of amazing things.

For example, improvements in navigation systems for commercial airliners came from NASA research. NASA-invented robots are being used to search for oil reserves far underneath the sea. Better contact lenses, ones that are less likely to harbor bacteria, came from NASA research. Farmers are getting tremendous help from NASA-developed hardware that tells them the right time to pick grapes and other crops. A system based on astronauts' space suits is in use to help athletes recover from injuries twice as fast as normal. The 360-degree virtual reality photography that we enjoy on the Internet was invented by NASA. These are just a few of the remarkable inventions that have come out of our space program and touch our everyday lives in positive ways.

I believe man should continue to explore space in an effort to make life better here on this planet. If I were president, I'd make sure that happened.

Much better, don't you think? Would you stop here and turn it in? Not yet—we're just getting warmed up! Let's tear this piece apart word by word, looking for any weakling we can find. It's time for some muscle!

A *really foolish idea*—not bad, but it could be even stronger. This is an opinion paper, so let's make the difference between the two sides clearer. Let's say that those people say it's unethical, even immoral, to spend billions of dollars . . .

They say . . . Say is such a weak word. It can mean so many things: whimper, confess, scream, cry, whisper. What are these people doing? Are they whispering? Surely not. Screaming? Probably not. Let's say they are arguing their point.

I believe their objections are wrong. Wrong is too weak. We can't just say "I'm right and they're wrong." We have to be clearer than that. I believe their objections, although well founded, don't consider the whole picture.

We should get to know more about our universe. Why? This is one of those sentences that sounds okay when you first read it, but in good writing, ask yourself the why question about every single sentence. If a sentence is too weak to make a clear point that someone would want to read, ax it. That's what we are going to do with this sentence. Bye bye, weak sentence.

Good technology has already come from the space program is too weak. Again, this is where the main point of this paper begins. It needs to be strong and clear. How about this: *An impressive amount of technology that has come out of the space program is already enriching our everyday lives, improving our healthcare system, promising environmentally clean oil exploration, and keeping us safer in the skies.*

To end the piece by saying *if I were president* and taking this idea no further is weak. The paper fizzles out, trails off into nowhere. If I wanted to write another paragraph about policies I'd implement as president, that would be fine. But I don't want to go in that direction. Instead, I'll rephrase my main idea in order to create a zingy ending.

After the third round of cleanup, this is what we have:

A recent survey indicates that 28% of the American population believes that it's foolish and even irresponsible for man to explore outer space. These people argue that it's unethical, even immoral, to spend billions of dollars for each mission of the space program when people here at home are in need of improvements in housing, education, and health care.

I believe their objections, although well founded, don't consider the whole picture. An impressive amount of technology that has come out of the space program is already enriching our everyday lives, improving our healthcare system, promising environmentally clean oil exploration, and keeping us safer in the skies.

For example, improvements in navigation systems for commercial airliners came from NASA research. NASA-invented robots are being used to search for oil reserves far underneath the sea. Better contact lenses, ones that are less likely to harbor bacteria, came from NASA research. Farmers are getting tremendous help from NASA-developed hardware that tells them the right time to pick grapes and other crops. A system based on astronauts' space suits is in use to help athletes recover from injuries twice as fast as normal. The 360-degree virtual reality photography that we enjoy on the Internet was invented by NASA. These are just a few of the remarkable inventions that have come out of our space program and touch our everyday lives in positive ways.

I believe man should continue to explore space. Whether we land on Mars, whether our children and grandchildren live in space stations thousands of miles away—perhaps those aren't the crucial points. Perhaps the best thing that the space program gives us is a fascinating way to continue to explore all parts of our universe in order to enrich life for everyone on this planet.

Finally! It took some work, and it took a lot of ruthless rooting out of the mistakes and the weaklings, but I think it turned out great. What do you think?

Index